THE DIVINITY SCHOOL
AND
DUKE HUMFREY'S LIBRARY
AT OXFORD

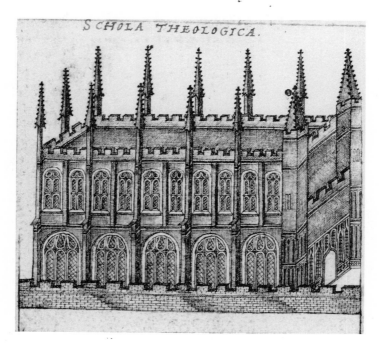

FRONTISPIECE. The Divinity School and Duke Humfrey's Library in 1566, from the north-west. By John Bereblock. (MS Bodley 13, fol. 16ᵛ)

FRONT COVER. The Divinity School, looking west. (Thomas–Photos, Oxford)
BACK COVER. Duke Humfrey's Library, looking west. (Thomas–Photos, Oxford)

THE DIVINITY SCHOOL
AND
DUKE HUMFREY'S LIBRARY
AT OXFORD

Stanley Gillam

Clarendon Press Oxford
in association with the Bodleian Library
1988

Oxford University Press, Walton Street, Oxford OX2 6DP

Oxford New York Toronto
Delhi Bombay Calcutta Madras Karachi
Petaling Jaya Singapore Hong Kong Tokyo
Nairobi Dar es Salaam Cape Town
Melbourne Auckland

and associated companies in
Beirut Berlin Ibadan Nicosia

Oxford is a trade mark of Oxford University Press

Published in the United States
by Oxford University Press, New York

British Library Cataloguing in Publication Data
Gillam, Stanley
The Divinity School and Duke Humfrey's Library at Oxford
1. Oxfordshire. Oxford. Universities. Colleges.
Libraries. Duke Humfrey's Library. Buildings.
Architectural features
I. Title   II. Bodleian Library
727'.82742574
ISBN 0-19-951558-1

Library of Congress Cataloging in Publication Data
Gillam, Stanley.
The Divinity School and Duke Humfrey's Library
at Oxford / by Stanley Gillam.
Includes index.
1. Bodleian Library.   2. Reading rooms—England—
Oxford (Oxfordshire)—History.   3. Libraries,
University and college—England—Oxford (Oxfordshire)—
History.   4. Humphrey, Duke of Gloucester, 1391–1447.
5. Library architecture—England—Oxford (Oxfordshire)
6. University of Oxford—Buildings—History.
7. Oxford (Oxfordshire)—Buildings, structures, etc.
8. Historic buildings—England—Oxford (Oxfordshire)
I. Title.
Z792.094G54 1988   027.7425'74-19   88–5321
ISBN 0-19-951558-1 (pbk.)

Printed in Great Britain by
The Alden Press Ltd., Oxford

FOREWORD

It is a rare privilege for a library to be able to celebrate the 500th anniversary of the opening of a reading room which it still occupies. We have that privilege at the Bodleian Library in 1988. The room is now known as Duke Humfrey's Library and it was added at a late stage to the Divinity School, whose construction had begun in the early 1420s. In 1488 it was open for use. It was subsequently refurnished and redecorated by Sir Thomas Bodley in the last years of the sixteenth century. The building serves no one College but belongs to the University of Oxford as a whole, and the two rooms inside it—the Divinity School and Duke Humfrey's Library—are the University's two chief early architectural treasures.

In this small book Stanley Gillam tells the fascinating story of the building's original construction, and of the problems posed at that time by the lack of adequate finances and by the elaborations of over-ambitious master masons. He goes on to sketch in the outlines of the subsequent history of the structure which the University's burgeoning collection of books has submitted to some extraordinary strains over the centuries and in doing so he has made it much easier for us to appreciate the building's beautiful and intricate details. He deserves our congratulations and thanks for presenting a complicated story so succinctly and at the same time making it so interesting. At many points the text acknowledges the research done on the early history of the building by Dr J. N. L. Myres, Bodley's Librarian from 1947 to 1965. Dr Myres's term of office coincided with the refurbishment and restoration of the Divinity School and Duke Humfrey's Library. Both Stanley Gillam and I are delighted here to acknowledge the outstanding contribution which Dr Myres has made over many years to the history of the splendid building whose quincentenary we now celebrate.

DAVID VAISEY
Bodley's Librarian

CONTENTS

ILLUSTRATIONS

ABBREVIATIONS

Annual Report	*Annual Report of the Curators of the Bodleian Library.*
BLR	*The Bodleian Library Record.* Vol. 1– . 1938– .
BQR	*The Bodleian Quarterly Record.* Vol. 1–8. 1914–38.
Bodley to James	G. W. Wheeler (ed.). *Letters of Sir Thomas Bodley to Thomas James, First Keeper of the Bodleian Library.* 1926.
Bodley to Univ.	G. W. Wheeler (ed.). *Letters of Sir Thomas Bodley to the University of Oxford 1598–1611.* 1927.
Cox	A. D. M. Cox, 'An account for the building of the Divinity School'. *Oxoniensia,* xxi (1956), 48–60.
Craster	Sir H. H. E. Craster. *History of the Bodleian Library 1845–1945.* 1952.
Emden	A. B. Emden. *A Biographical Register of the University of Oxford to AD 1500.* 3 vols. 1957–9.
Ep. Acad.	H. Anstey (ed.). *Epistolae Academicae Oxon. (Registrum F).* 2 pts. (OHS 35, 36.) 1898.
Hope	Sir W. St John Hope. 'The heraldry and sculpture of the vault of the Divinity School at Oxford'. *Archaeological Journal,* lxxi (1914), 217–60.
Legge	H. E. Legge. *The Divinity School: A Guide for Visitors.* 1923.
Macray	W. D. Macray. *Annals of the Bodleian Library, Oxford.* 2nd edn. 1890.
Med. Arch.	H. E. Salter (ed.). *Mediaeval Archives of the University of Oxford.* Vol. ii. (OHS 73.) 1921.
Mun. Acad.	H. Anstey (ed.). *Munimenta Academica, or Documents Illustrative of the Academical Life and Studies in Oxford.* 2 pts. (Rolls series.) 1868.
Myres	J. N. L. Myres. 'Recent discoveries in the Bodleian Library'. *Archaeologia,* ci (1967), 150–68.
OHS	Oxford Historical Society.
Philip	I. G. Philip, *The Bodleian Library in the Seventeenth and Eighteenth Centuries.* 1983.
Pietas	*Pietas Oxoniensis: In Memory of Sir Thomas Bodley, knt. and the Foundation of the Bodleian Library.* 1902.
Poole	Mrs R. L. Poole. *Catalogue of Portraits in the Possession of the University, Colleges, City and County of Oxford.* 3 vols. (OHS 57, 81, 82.) 1911–26.

Reg. Canc.	H. E. Salter (ed.). *Registrum Cancellarii Oxoniensis, 1434–69.* 2 vols. (OHS 93, 94.) 1932.
Reg. Cong.	W. A. Pantin and W. T. Mitchell (eds.). *The Register of Congregation 1448–1463.* With an Epilogue by G. Pollard. (OHS NS 22.) 1972.
RCHM	Royal Commission on Historical Monuments. *An Inventory of the Historical Monuments in the City of Oxford.* 1939.
SC	*A Summary Catalogue of Western Manuscripts in the Bodleian Library.* 7 vols. [in 8]. 1895–1953.
Statuta	S. Gibson (ed.). *Statuta Antiqua Universitatis Oxoniensis.* 1931.
Trecentale	*Trecentale Bodleianum: A Memorial Volume.* 1913.
VCH	Victoria County History. *Oxfordshire.* Vol. iii. 1954.
Wood, *Hist.*	A. Wood. *The History and Antiquities of the University of Oxford*, ed. J. Gutch. 2 vols. [in 3]. 1792–6.
Wood, *Life*	A. Clark (ed.). *The Life and Times of Anthony Wood.* 5 vols. (OHS 19, 21, 26, 30, 40.) 1891–1900.

SOURCES

Contemporary documents relating to the planning and building of the Divinity School and Duke Humfrey's Library at Oxford are few in number. Apart from one roll of accounts, which is among the muniments of University College, they are all in the University Archives. By far the most important manuscript for the historian of the building is known as Registrum F which contains copies of letters and other documents relating to the administration of the University from 1421 to 1508. It has been printed in full, with an introduction by the editor, Henry Anstey, and is referred to below as *Ep. Acad.* Anstey has provided English summaries of many of the documents therein and has suggested that the Register was called 'F' after John Farley who copied some of the documents into it. Graham Pollard, however, has pointed out that many hands appear in the volume including those of sixteen successive Registrars.[1] Other copies of some of the letters, together with one which is not in Registrum F, are to be found in MS Corpus Christi College, Cambridge 423.[2]

The Proctors' Accounts, which record year by year the sums which they received and expended on behalf of the University, are to be found in print in *Med. Arch.*, VOL. ii. There are entries in these accounts relating to the building but, unfortunately, the rolls for many of the relevant years have not survived. Other documents and registers from the University Archives will be found in *Mun. Acad., Reg. Canc.*, and *Reg. Cong.* The single document among the University College muniments is an account kept by William Churche, supervisor of the building, of money spent on it during the period July 1452 to December 1453. It has been published by A. D. M. Cox and is referred to as *Cox.*

INTRODUCTION

THE University of Oxford was originally an ecclesiastical body. In its earliest days it came under the jurisdiction of the bishops of Lincoln in whose diocese it then was. It is not surprising, therefore, that the University Church of St Mary the Virgin became not only the centre of administration but also the repository for such manuscripts as the University corporately possessed. These were kept in a chest (*Antiqua cista librorum*), were highly valued, and were reserved exclusively for the use of senior members of the University.[1]

The first University library as such was founded by Thomas Cobham, Bishop of Worcester. It formed the upper storey of the Congregation House adjoining St Mary's Church on the north side, which Cobham began to build in 1320 and which was the first building to be owned by the University as a corporate body.[2] Cobham died seven years later and bequeathed to the University both money and books, but so heavy were his debts that the latter had to be pawned to pay his funeral expenses. They were acquired by Adam de Brome, Rector of St Mary's, and placed in the library of the new hall which he had recently founded and which later became Oriel College. In 1337, five years after Brome's death, the University managed to regain possession of its books, though not without difficulty, and the dispute with the College was not finally settled until 1410.[3] Having retrieved its books, however, the University was not yet in a position properly to house them. For the time being they were kept in two chests probably in the Congregation House.[4] Authorities differ regarding the date when the room over the House finally came into use as the University Library but 1367 seems to be the most likely.[5] In 1412 a new code of statutes governing the Library was drawn up among which was the provision that the Chancellor and the Proctors should check once a year that the Librarian was fit in morals, fidelity, and ability to continue to carry out his duties efficiently.[6]

By the beginning of the fifteenth century the University had lost much of the vigour of its earlier days. Its enthusiasms had waned and its numbers had declined, but it was during this period that Humfrey, Duke of Gloucester, the youngest son of Henry IV, made his magnificent gifts of books to the Library, numbering in all at least 281 volumes. His final donation in 1444 was so splendid that it moved the University to offer to build a new library over the Divinity School, then under construction, and to name it after him. More than forty years were to pass, however, after Humfrey's death before it was ready to receive the books. By that time the promise to perpetuate his name had been forgotten. Not until the nineteenth century was the description 'Duke Humfrey's Library' applied to the place in which his books had rested for only sixty-two years. Until 1907 it was the sole reading-room (apart from reserved seats elsewhere for those holding high office in the University) in the Bodleian building. It then began to be known as the Old Reading Room (a second room having been opened in that year), a name superseded only in recent times by the now familiar 'Duke Humfrey'. The quincentenary of the opening of surely one of the most beautiful library rooms in the world is now, in this year 1988, both commemorated and celebrated in the pages which follow.

I

The Divinity School and
Duke Humfrey's Library,
1423–1488

IT IS not possible to say precisely when the construction of the Divinity School actually began but the University of Oxford was soliciting donations for a new school of theology as early as 1423. In that year Congregation, the governing body of the University, wrote to their Chancellor, John Castell, asking him to endeavour to obtain payment from a person (unnamed) who had promised a contribution towards the project.[1] In April 1424 a letter was sent to Nicholas Bubwith, Bishop of Bath and Wells, begging for assistance, but he died in the following year and there is no record that he responded. From this letter, however, it could be assumed that some form of work, possibly the digging of the foundations, was already in progress because there is a reference to certain building of schools now begun.[2]

During the next five years a number of appeals were made for funds and it is interesting to note that the University cast its net in several directions. The executors of a certain John Whytynton were asked for help in 1424.[3] His name is not to be found in the reference books and it is not beyond the bounds of possibility that the forename was incorrectly recorded. It may be pure coincidence, however, that the famous Richard Whittington, thrice mayor of London, who contributed to building projects in his lifetime, including a library for the Grey Friars, and instructed his executors to found a college in London after his death, died in 1423.[4] The members of the Benedictine Order, assembled in their general Chapter at Northampton in 1426, were presented with a petition conveyed, on behalf of the University, by Edmund Kirton, the Prior of Gloucester Hall.[5] They were informed that the building of a School of Theology had begun but could not be completed because of lack of funds. As an inducement to contribute they were told that all their graduates and scholars would be free to use the School building.[6] It was four years before any money was forthcoming from them. One hundred pounds were promised and there are recorded receipts for part of this sum: 20 marks[7] from Ralph, Abbot of Abingdon,[8] a like amount from John Whethamstede, Abbot of St Albans,[9] both in 1430, and a further 50 marks from the latter in 1431.[10] In 1444 another letter was sent to the Benedictines thanking them for the money already subscribed and asking for the remainder of the promised sum.[11] Presumably this request related to the sum of £100 promised at least fourteen years earlier but there seems to have been no reply.

There was a concentrated effort in 1426 to obtain donations towards the new School. Stock letters were drafted[12] and copies were sent out to bishops, deans and chapters, and others. Salisbury, Bath and Wells, Exeter, and Lincoln[13] are known to have been approached, as was the Chapter of the Augustinian Friars,[14] but none seems to have responded. Donations were, however, received from the Archbishop of Canterbury, Henry Chichele,[15] and the Dean of St Paul's, Reginald Kentwode.[16] An interesting letter was sent to the Master of St Thomas's Hospital, London, the gist of which was 'your labours for our welfare could not be the greater had you been educated here; we therefore confidently beg that you will intercede for us with wealthy citizens of London, that they may assist us in building the new schools, and that you will advise our Chancellor how to cast his net on the right side of the ship, when he appeals to them for assistance.'[17] An appeal to Thomas Langley, Bishop of Durham, in 1428,[18] which produced a donation for which he was thanked in 1430[19] seems to have ended the current fund-raising campaign but money was undoubtedly in short supply. In the latter year the University decreed that half of the money received for the granting of graces should be applied to the building of the School.[20]

If preparations for building had, in fact, been made in 1423 very little can have been done in the three succeeding years because the University in 1426 thanked Henry Chichele for his gift 'by which progress may more happily surround the newly begun foundations of our schools'.[21] Whatever went on in these early days, however, the ground upon which the School was to stand was not formally acquired until 1427. By a deed dated 6 July in that year[22] the University obtained from Balliol College on a 99-year lease a piece of land on which formerly stood St Hugh's Hall, bounded by Exeter

College on the west, School Street[23] on the east, Exeter Lane, running alongside the city wall on the north, and some tenements belonging to the Abbot and Convent of Dorchester and to Balliol College on the south. In return the University leased to Balliol Sparrow Hall, also known as Old Balliol Hall, adjoining the College on the north side of what is now Broad Street.[24] In addition the University acquired another piece of land which belonged to St Frideswide's Priory, on which once stood St Patrick's Hall, at an annual rent of 3s. 4d.[25] The Chancellor of the University from 1426 to 1431 was Thomas Chace, Master of Balliol from 1412 to 1422, and the scheme for the erection of the Divinity School owed much to his energy and influence. As Chancellor he was a party to the deeds between the University and his own college and it is tempting to think that the loan which he raised the day before their execution (and again on 14 May 1434), as security for which he deposited a Balliol College book in the Winton Chest (now MS Bodley 252), was destined for the building fund. He later became chaplain to Duke Humfrey and was nominated by the University to assist the Chancellor in the negotiations arising from the Duke's final gift of books in 1444. He is not commemorated on the vault of the building but it is surely significant that his shield of arms is carved in stone on the lowest stage of the ends of the buttresses of the north wall where the building operation began.[26]

The Divinity School must originally have been designed as a single-storey hall of five bays. The substantial buttresses between these bays imply an intention that it should be vaulted, though the vault would most naturally have sprung from a higher point on the walls and would have risen to a greater height than is now the case.[27] There were to be windows in each bay, as today, and also two flanking the doorways at the east and west ends of the School. At some point during the period of building the recesses of the latter were blocked up but traces of them may still be seen at the east end as one enters the School from the Proscholium. On the inside at both ends of the room the blind window openings were skilfully adapted to fit in with the vaulting in 1480. There must presumably have been an architect or overseer in charge of the work in the early stages but there is no record of his name. In August 1430, however, the University decided to appoint a master mason, Richard Winchcombe, as supervisor. He was not an Oxford man and had hitherto carried out very little work locally. He was in charge of the building of the chancel of Adderbury Church, Oxfordshire in 1408–1418, he was employed for a week on the pinnacles of New College in 1412/13, for which he was paid 3s. 3d., and he may have done some work at Balliol.[28] His terms of appointment were clearly laid down:

To all the faithful of Christ who shall see these present letters, the Chancellor of the University of Oxford and the University itself greeting: Know that we have granted to master Richard Wynchecombe, mason, a pension of forty shillings sterling to be paid yearly at the feasts of St. Michael the archangel and of Easter by equal portions, so long as he stay and continue to survey the work of the new schools of theology in the said University; also a gown of the livery of gentlemen every year, or thirteen shillings and fourpence for the same; and every week when he shall be present at the work in the same place four shillings sterling for his pay. Also the said master Richard shall have a proper house for himself and his mates, and hay enough for one horse, when the same Richard shall be present at the same work, at the costs of the said University; and he shall also have reasonable expenses, as often as he shall be sent upon the business of the said University.[29]

The years following Winchcombe's appointment saw a sad decline in the state of the University. Money was short, the number of students had declined, graduates could not find employment and buildings were falling into decay. In 1437, the year in which the School's most generous later benefactor, Thomas Kempe, was Proctor, a Chest of Three Keys was instituted to keep separate the money earmarked for the building of it.[30] No record of the progress of the work has survived but it must have been rather slow. This was not entirely due, however, to the restraining hand of poverty; Winchcombe favoured elaborate ornamentation of the stonework. By 1439 the University had become impatient and Winchcombe was replaced. Nothing is known of his successor, Thomas Elkyn, except that he perhaps came from Barrington in the Cotswolds, that he had a tenement in Cat Street, and that he died in 1449.[31] His terms of appointment, dated 6 January 1439/40, were considerably less favourable than those of his predecessor. It is possible that his professional standing was not as high and that the University wished to economise on the salary of their employee. He was told to eliminate unnecessary ornamentation and 'frivolous curiosities' which were expensive, time-consuming, and lacking in taste:

This indenture made between the University of Oxford on the one part and Thomas Elkyn, mason, on the other part, witnesses that the said Thomas has undertaken the building of the new schools of divinity in the University aforesaid in so much as pertains to masonry; and the aforesaid Thomas shall receive weekly through the summer four shillings sterling and through the winter three shillings and four pence when it happens that he himself is so working there weekly in person

Also the said Thomas shall introduce other masons, the best whom he knows and at the best price he can, for the profit of the said work; but their number shall be according to the will of the surveyors of the said work

And the said Thomas shall receive from the same University yearly in the said work a mark sterling for his pension

And because many great people of the realm and other wise men do not approve, but censure, too much curiosity of the said work, therefore the said University wills that the said Thomas hold back in future, as he has begun to hold back, such superfluous curiosity of the said work, namely in the housings of images . . . casements and fillets and other frivolous curiosities, which are not to the point and involve the University in costly expenses and the delaying of the work

And for faithfully holding and observing the said agreements on the part of the said Thomas, the same Thomas binds himself to the said University in £40 sterling[32]

One of the results of the instruction to Elkyn to adopt a plainer style of building has made it possible for later generations to assess with some degree of accuracy how much progress had been made by 1440. It is clear that the north wall had risen to a much greater height than the south because the buttresses are panelled on that side to a point half-way up the present windows of Duke Humfrey's Library. The wall would, of course, have been blank at that point because no upper room was planned at that time. On the south side the buttresses are not panelled above the plinth and the mouldings are more simple in the windows that had not been finished at the time of Elkyn's appointment. If one looks at the reveal of the easternmost window of the School on the south side the contrast will be seen between the elaborate work of Winchcombe and the simpler style of Elkyn (Ill. 1). It is reasonable, therefore, to assume that by 1440 the south wall had not risen much above the plinth which is panelled and decorated as on the north side. The exterior of the west doorway, which today leads into the seventeenth-century Convocation House, is decorated in Winchcombe's style. This was revealed when

1. The south-east window of the Divinity School showing the contrast between the elaborate work of Richard Winchcombe (before 1439) and the simpler style of Thomas Elkyn (1439–49). (Thomas-Photos, Oxford)

panelling in the House was removed during restoration work early in the 1960s (Ill. 2). It has been suggested that the idea of a vaulted roof was abandoned at the same time as the other economies were introduced.[33] If so, this would explain why the northern buttresses, except for the uppermost stage, were bonded to the walls, preparatory to taking the weight of a vault, whereas those on the south side were not so constructed when the work went ahead under Elkyn's direction. The picture, therefore, in 1440 would seem to be of an empty shell of a single-storey building with a north wall nearing roof level, east and west walls, each with a doorway, well advanced in

2. The exterior of the west doorway of the Divinity School revealed during restoration work. The elaborate detail indicates that it was constructed before 1439. (Thomas-Photos, Oxford)

height, but with a south wall rising only a few feet above ground level.

There is no record of what progress was made during the next three years or so but in 1444 there occurred an event which was radically to change the building plans, such as they were. Humfrey, Duke of Gloucester, who had already made several donations of books to the University Library, now came forward with a further gift so large and so outstanding that a mere expression of thanks, however fulsome, was considered inadequate. Something more lasting was required on this occasion and the University rose to it. Their letter of gratitude, filled with superlatives, may be summarized thus:

By your magnificent donation, from having been well-nigh without books, this University has become richer than any other in these treasures; so that we scarcely know where to bestow them. . . . Our words are too feeble to express our thanks, and we wish for a permanent memorial of your generosity. If we could place your books in a suitable chamber, separate from others, the crowding of the readers might be avoided; and for this purpose we would offer the new school now in building. The situation is retired and quiet, and we venture to suggest that the new library should be called by your name.[34]

Dr Myres has suggested that this letter may have been drafted by Thomas Chaundeler, the Junior Proctor in 1444, and that the idea of building a library over the School may have been his. He was a scholar of Winchester and during his time there a small chapel with a library over, known as Fromond's Chantry, was being constructed in the cloisters. The upper room was reached, as with Duke Humfrey, by a turret staircase at the west end. Chaundeler would have had this small building clearly in mind when, as Proctor, he was closely involved in the plan for a similar structure in Oxford. In later years he continued to play a part in the slow process of completing it, both as Vice-Chancellor and as Chancellor, and he is commemorated in several places on the Divinity School vault.[35]

It is evident that the University's offer met with the duke's approval, for, shortly before his death in 1447, he promised yet another gift of books and the sum of £100 towards the cost of building the new room.[36] Unfortunately this promise was never fulfilled and neither the books nor the money ever found their way to Oxford. Nevertheless one must assume that the work went ahead.

The proposed additional storey above the Divinity School created the need for decisions on a number of vital points such as the height of the walls, the level of the floor between the two rooms, the provision of windows in the upper storey and the means of access to it. But decisions were *not* made. Nearly a decade of delay and uncertainty followed, complicated by the death of Thomas Elkyn in 1449, but the financial situation improved in the mean while. On 5 February 1448 the University sent a letter to John Kempe, then Archbishop of York, the chief executor of Cardinal Beaufort who had died in the preceding year, begging him to move his colleagues to grant something towards the building fund.[37] The outcome was a contribution of 500 marks, not, however, entirely free of conditions.[38] One was that the money should be repaid if the building was not finished within five years, the actual date specified being 1 March 1453, and another that the money would not be paid over unless certain persons of standing in the University made themselves personally responsible for its return if the first condition was not fulfilled. It was difficult to find graduates willing to commit themselves to this obligation but eventually the Chancellor, Gilbert Kymer, and Elias Holcote, Warden of Merton, agreed to serve on condition that the University would promise to indemnify them against loss. This assurance was given and the University at once proceeded to elect a body of twelve commissioners to find ways and means of completing the fabric within the stipulated five years and to ensure that Kymer and Holcote were given the necessary security. The commission was to consist of the Chancellor, the two Proctors, and nine other graduates. They met soon after appointment and drew up a set of regulations which are summarized below. There were to be twelve deputy commissioners (who are named) and two supervisors of the building works. Rules were laid down for the organization of existing funds and also for obtaining additional money. It is interesting to note that the commissioners did not shrink from such measures as advocating the sale of graces, bribing would-be donors with the offer of indulgences, and relaxing the statutes in favour of religious societies.

REGULATIONS

Deputy commissioners, to serve in case of the inability of the commissioners, are appointed

Two Masters of Arts are to be appointed to act as superintendents of the works during the building; to engage and pay the workmen employed, &c. They shall render an account of all moneys which they shall receive, and they shall be bound by oath to the faithful discharge of these duties

They shall each receive a salary of four marks yearly

They shall be removeable from their office by the twelve commissioners

One such superintendent only shall suffice, if the commissioners shall think fit

Two superintendents are appointed subject to the above regulations

All other sums of money given by the University, to supplement the said five hundred marks, shall be in charge of the guardians of the chest of five keys and delivered in instalments by them to the superintendents

None of the moneys, given or raised howsoever for the erection of the said schools, shall come into the hands of the Proctors

No sums shall be paid to the superintendents of the works from the chest of five keys, except by the express consent of the commissioners, and then only under an indenture

To raise additional funds for the completion of the building, Congregation shall be allowed to grant graces, with certain restrictions, upon payment of certain sums by the persons seeking such graces

The University shall write to the King to ask for materials for the said building, and also to ecclesiastics both secular and religious, especially to such as are graduates, to ask for money

Indulgences shall also be sought from the Pope and bishops for those who give money

All non-resident Doctors and Masters shall pay eight pence, and all Bachelors four pence, a year to the University

Executors of wealthy persons deceased shall be asked for benefactions

Fines levied by the University shall be applied to the purposes of the aforesaid building

The offer of one hundred pounds by certain religious societies, on condition of a relaxation of the statutes in their favour, shall be accepted

A further offer from the same shall also be accepted[39]

The first two supervisors appointed by the commissioners were John Evelyn, one of their own number, Rector of Exeter College 1443–9, and William Leyley, one of the deputies, but Leyley died soon afterwards and was replaced by Robert Cowper, another of the commissioners.[40] Evelyn left Oxford in the autumn of 1451 to become Minister, Canon and Prebendary of Ottery St Mary[41] and Cowper died on 8 June 1452.[42] Thereafter it seems that only one supervisor was deemed necessary and William Churche, Principal of Brasenose Hall, filled the post until about the end of 1457.[43] It is not exactly clear when Beaufort's legacy became available. Some of it must have been in the University's hands well in advance of the qualifying date stipulated by the executors by which the building was to be finished. Certainly the whole amount had been received by 1453 and almost entirely spent, because in May of that year the accounts kept by the trustees, Kymer and Holcote, were audited. The auditors certified that the sum bequeathed had been properly paid to, and spent by, the supervisors Evelyn and Cowper, on the purposes intended and that a balance of £2 10s. 4d. remained.[44]

The supervisors, however, were responsible not only for spending the money allocated for building but also for helping to collect it. One of their duties was to visit the executors of wealthy persons as laid down in the Regulations, bearing letters of supplication for assistance. In 1449 Cowper called upon Thomas Lesurs,[45] Dean of St Paul's, who was an executor of Walter Shyrryntone, and upon the executors of John Gedney, a London man.[46] There is no record that he had any success. It is likely that Churche went in person to Gilbert Kymer, then Dean of Salisbury, in 1453, with a letter requesting a loan of £10, and to the executors of William Alnwick, lately Bishop of Lincoln, by whom he was given £10.[47] Kymer's loan was still outstanding in 1454 when the University wrote to him again apologizing for the delay in repayment and asking for an even larger sum.[48] The quest for help continued. A letter to Edmund Rede in 1453, who had already given timber towards the building, asked for a donation of some stone.[49] He seems to have suggested that an approach to Lord Lovell might bear fruit and a letter was duly sent to him.[50] With an appeal to the executors of Rawlyn Holand[51] and a donation of £20 from the Duchess of Suffolk in 1454 the drive for financial help ceased for the time being.[52] Both of these begging letters were borne by the supervisor, Churche.

It is difficult to assess what stage the building had reached by 1452, the year in which Churche was appointed, but a contemporary record exists of the money received and expended by him from July 1452 until December 1453[53] (Ill. 3). The total sum allocated to him from various sources during the eighteen months covered by the account amounted to £51 5s. 4d. included in which was the figure of £2 10s. 4d. noted by the auditors of the Beaufort legacy as being unspent. Much of the Beaufort money must have been used up before Churche's appointment but one of the first things he did was to take definite steps to settle once and for all the vital points which had for so long been left undecided. Two experienced craftsmen were called in to survey and settle the height of the building, involving also, as it must have done, decisions about the floor level of the library room and the position and size of its windows. Robert Jannyns of Abingdon,[54] who had previously been involved in work at All Souls and Merton, and John Atkyns, who had also worked at Merton,[55] took only two days to make their recommendations. They were allowed expenses of 12*d.* in addition to their fees of 4*s.* Quantities of stone were obtained from Burford, Headington, and Taynton, timber from Stow Wood, possibly for flooring or roofing (although there is nothing to suggest that this had begun), and reeds from Binsey to make a temporary thatch for protecting the walls. These must have reached a fair height because Churche's account includes expenditure on 'scafold tymbur' and there is mention of a 'magna rota', a large crane worked by a tread-wheel. By the end of 1453 the building must have reached a point at which it was almost ready to receive the roof but the building account showed a deficit of nearly £20, £70 4*s.* 6*d.* having been spent in the eighteen months covered by it.

A further period of comparative inactivity followed, caused probably by overspending and lack of funds. No record of expenditure exists until 1457 when the sum of 4 nobles [56] was taken from the Proctors' Chest for some form of roofing,[57] and a grant of £10 (to be repaid) was made from the Chest of Five Keys in 1458.[58] The first of the surviving rolls of Proctors' Accounts [59] records an outlay in 1464/5 of 16*d.* on straw for covering the walls probably to keep them dry or as a protection against frost,[60] and 3*s.* 6*d.* for labour.[61] Dr. Myres has suggested that the straw was for a thatched roof,[62] but Dr Salter thought otherwise. He pointed out that the sum involved was insufficient to pay for a roof and that the walls were, in any case, unfinished.[63] In 1465 also a begging letter was sent to the executors of Thomas Beckington, lately Bishop of Bath and Wells, the burden of which was that various repairs and the building of the new School had entirely exhausted the University's funds, and that the pinch of poverty had never before been felt so keenly. No response is on record but as the Bishop's coat of arms appears twice on the vault of the Divinity School it is possible that he or his executors made some contribution towards the building of it.[64] There item   The aforesaid supervisor desires that there should be allocated from the four shillings paid to John Atkyns and Robert Jannyns of Abingdon for their remuneration, for overseeing and marking out the height of the said structure of the new schools   4s.

item   To their expenses in staying in the town for two days   12d.

item   To cement for the repair of the stones   6d.

item   To one bucket for the carrying of water   8d.

item   Paid to John Danyell of Stanton St John for the carriage of timber given by the King at Stow Wood for the same schools   26s. 8d.

item   To expenses at Headington Quarry in the matter of selection of good stones, for the workmen in that place   4d.

item   To staves for the repair of the great wheel   4d.

item   On the Thursday next after the Feast of St Michael the Archangel to Robert the quarryman for the preparation and disposal of stones at Headington Quarry   4d.

item   To expenses in respect of John Atkyns in communicating to the quarrymen of Taynton the dimensions of stones to be sent   2d.

---

3. Part of the building account of William Churche showing payments, among others, to Robert Jannyns and John Atkyns. (University College muniments)

[15]

are no Proctors' Accounts extant for the period from April 1465 until April 1469, but some money must have been available because in June 1466 the University entered into a contract with a certain John Godard to make 37 desks with benches for the School which were to be ready by November. There must, therefore, have been some sort of roof on the building by this time. The terms of the contract are interesting:

On the feast of St. Barnabas the apostle, namely the eleventh day of June, John Godard of Bucklebury in the county of Berks 'hosbandman' bound himself to make desks with forms for the new schools of Sacred Theology at Oxford; namely, thirty-seven desks with corresponding benches of the form and fashion discussed in the same schools in the presence of doctor Calbek, master William Lampton, master John Byrde, and master J. Arnold, also of master Richard Mey and of me, Thomas Chaundeler, commissary general of the University of Oxford: so that the same work be fully, perfectly, and well finished according to the form and fashion aforesaid before the feast of St. Andrew next ensuing [1 November] under pain of £40 sterling to be paid to the aforesaid University. These things were done in the presence of us Thomas Chaundeler the commissary aforesaid the above mentioned eleventh day of June AD 1466 in the presence of doctor Cokkys, master John Molyneux, and master John Arnold; for which he shall receive £22 in part payment of which he now receives beforehand 100s. at the hands of master Richard Mey, vicar of the Church of St Helen Abingdon.[65]

The heads of the desks were not carved until 1469/70 when the Proctors' Accounts show an outlay of £2 6s. 8d. on this work; also £10 on finishing a wall and £3 for glazing windows.[66] It is difficult to reconcile expenditure of this kind with the contents of letters sent out by the University in 1470. In June George Nevill, Archbishop of York and Chancellor of the University, was asked to bring pressure to bear on Richard Mey, Vicar of St Helen's, Abingdon (already mentioned in the contract for the desks) to speed the payment of a promised donation.[67] A month later a fulsome letter went to the vicar saying that scarcely anyone else had been found to take pity on the poverty of the University and but for his generosity the new School of theology could not have been built.[68] Four months after that a heart-rending plea went to Walter Lyhart, Bishop of Norwich: 'our new School remains unfinished and unless you can help us we do not know how it can ever be completed.' The letter goes on to say that until a new library is provided there is no proper place in which to house a large bequest of books recently received from the late John Tiptoft, Earl of Worcester.[69] One letter implied that the building was virtually complete and the other that, without more money, that happy position would never be reached.

The state of the building in 1470, as in previous years, can only be conjectural. It must have had some form of roof in order to house the desks which had been bought earlier, but, as Dr Myres has pointed out, probably neither roof, walls nor windows reached their final height for another decade. The turret staircases at the west end, providing access to the upper floor, almost certainly were unfinished and there are no references to them in any of the available documents. Very few expenses of any sort are recorded in the Proctors' Accounts from 1470 onwards: in 1471/2, 29s. 8d. for repairs to walls and roof[70] and 8s. for repairs to the windows;[71] in 1472/3, 3s. for cleaning the School, for closing (presumably either glazing or shuttering) the upper windows, and for blocking up certain holes, possibly those used for scaffold poles,[72] and 26s. 8d. for repairs to the leadwork of the roof;[73] and in 1474/5 the large sum of £14 13s. 4d. for repairs done or to be done to the School, together with 26s. 8d. for the supervisor.[74] It is clear that work had slowed down again and that routine maintenance was necessary to prevent the building from falling into disrepair, but no further expenditure on it appears in the accounts during the next three years.

In 1478 means were found to bring this unhappy and unsatisfactory state of affairs to an end. The University decided to make another appeal, this time to Thomas Kempe, Bishop of London, and at last they found a benefactor whose generosity ensured that the new Divinity School, with Duke Humfrey's Library over it, would in due time be finally completed. The appeal letter,[75] which was conveyed to the Bishop by Thomas Karver of Magdalen College, for which service he was paid 20s.,[76] stressed the poverty of the University and its inability to complete the School which, after many years, was still unfinished and somewhat neglected. Kempe was invited to undertake the task, one which no ordinary man could contemplate, and his name would be for ever associated with it, as that of Solomon with the Temple at Jerusalem. Within a short time he had signified his good intentions to Thomas Chaundeler, the Chancellor of the University, who, in a letter dated 12 February 1478 conveyed the news to Convocation. The University hastened to write again to the bishop intimating that in return for his donation, which was to be the princely sum of 1,000 marks, they would be happy to comply with any condition attached to it.[77] He had stipulated that there should be an annual commemoration service for the souls of his deceased uncle John Kempe, Cardinal Archbishop of Canterbury, who died in 1454, and of himself after his own death. This was promised on the understanding that the 1,000 marks should be paid over first.[78] The necessary statute, having received the bishop's approval, was duly passed in Congregation in September 1478[79] and in the same month the University entered into an indenture with him incorporating this agreement and setting out the conditions governing the payment of the donation and of the uses to which it was to be put.[80] Two hundred marks were to be paid at the date of the indenture, 3 September 1478, and two hundred more every year on the feast of All Saints until all were paid, to be applied to the completion of the new Divinity School and to no other purpose, and any money remaining after its completion was to be placed in the Kempe Chest for the support of poor scholars. (It is interesting to note that thirty years after the decision was taken to build an upper room which was to be Duke Humfrey's Library the building was still referred to simply as a School). The first instalment of 200 marks was duly paid over on the same day as the indenture was signed and the last in March 1482 but not quite as arranged. Seven payments were made in all, totalling 1,100 marks—four of 200 and three of 100.[81]

Interesting sidelights on the negotiations arising from Bishop Kempe's donation are to be found in the Proctors' Accounts for 1478/9, and these may best be expressed in the words of Dr Salter:

We read of a journey to Hinksey where the Chancellor, the Commissary, and many others treated about the intention of the Bishop of London to complete the School of Theology. If it is asked why the meeting was at Hinksey, the answer may be that the itinerant judges had to be consulted. There is an entry that the Proctors journeyed to Hinksey to obtain the goodwill of the judges, probably the itinerant judges for Berkshire, who usually held their court in that part of Grampound which was in Berkshire, in the parish of Hinksey. Two horses were hired at a cost of 12d. to visit the Chancellor about the oath of William Orchard; evidently the Chancellor was not far away, and as there is evidence that this was a year of severe plague he may have been in a neighbouring village. William Orchard is known to have been the architect and builder of much of Magdalen College, and the evidence is increasing which shows that he was the architect of all the chief buildings of Oxford that were erected between 1460 and 1504, the date of his death. There can be little doubt that the initials W.O., which occur more than once on the roof of the Divinity School, stand for William Orchard. We do not know why an oath was required from him; perhaps the Bishop of London desired that he should take an oath to complete the work within a certain date.[82]

The impetus given to the work by Kempe's donation was immediate, and austerity became a thing of the past, but the University continued to plead poverty, and other problems had to be overcome. William Waynflete, Bishop of Winchester, who was just completing Magdalen College, was asked to lend scaffolding because if the University itself had to provide it it would be a great drain on its resources and would seriously delay the completion of the work.[83] There was also a shortage of workmen because King Edward IV was employing so many at St George's Chapel, Windsor. The University wrote to him on 14 February 1479 saying that while they would not wish him to part with any of the men then at Windsor they hoped he would permit the employment of those who had been working on Magdalen College for Bishop Waynflete if the bishop would agree to lend them.[84] The Proctors' Accounts record that John Boswell, the beadle, was paid 20s. for conveying this letter to the king.[85]

We must now consider how this large donation affected the plans for completing the building. The decision to insert a vaulted ceiling in the Divinity School, an idea abandoned many years before, involved making major changes to some of the work already in position. The appointment of a competent architect was vital to the success of a very complicated operation and there is little doubt that the man chosen was William Orchard. That he was closely involved is clear from references to him in the Proctors' Accounts which have been mentioned above, and to these can be added another. In 1482/3 he was paid expenses of 13s. 4d. for travelling to see the Bishop of London.[86] The reason for the visit surely would have been to discuss the progress of the building, or perhaps the vault in particular, for which the bishop was paying.

While it is obvious that payments towards the building during this, or any earlier, period of construction, did not stem only from the Proctors' Chest it is unfortunate that their Accounts for the years between April 1483 and April 1488 have not survived and equally so that no other contemporary documents exist which throw any light upon the closing years of a long-drawn-out saga. The history of these final years, therefore, can only be deduced from the discoveries made in the course of the restoration work carried out in Duke Humfrey's Library and the adjacent rooms in the early 1960s which have been described by Dr Myres.[87] Up until the time of Bishop Kempe's donation the Divinity School had had a flat roof or ceiling. The proposal to introduce a vault, involving the need for more height, called for a complete reappraisal of the levels and proportions of the library room above—of floor, walls, windows, and roof. The vault itself had to be designed in such a way that it fitted round the splendid windows of the north and south walls of the School and the existing features of the east and west ends. It was under construction by August 1480, though not finished, as we know from William Worcestre who was in Oxford at that time and obtained measurements of the building which, in most respects, were fairly accurate.[88] The upper face of the vault, revealed during the 1960s restoration, has low arches which provide flat surfaces on which it was planned, presumably, that the main timbers of the library floor should rest. It must be remembered that the floor was not designed to take the weight which Bodley later imposed upon it. The original floorcases were neither so tall nor so heavy as those of today and they housed fewer books. Moreover, if the timbers were let into, or secured in some way to, the side walls the pressure on the vault below would not have been excessive. This floor had now to be higher than originally proposed in consequence of which the existing stone window-sills in the upper room rose very little above it. The original windows were designed, probably in 1452, in relation to a floor set at a lower level than that now required (Ill. 4a). Most of the window corbels, fashioned by several different workmen with their own individual styles, and still in place today, appear to belong to the third quarter of the fifteenth century. There are forty of them, twenty on each side, the majority of which are carved heads. The varying treatment of the eyes in the heads indicates that at least three different

4. Suggested elevation of one bay on the north side of the building (a) as proposed in 1452 and (b) as built after the insertion of the Divinity School vault in 1480. (Drawing by Robert Potter)

Scale ⊢┈⊢┈┈┈┈┈┈⊣ Feet

craftsmen were employed. To use Dr Myres's terminology, some have 'lentoid' eyes, some slit eyes, and others 'drilled' eyes. On the north wall, 11 are lentoid, 4 are drilled, and 3 are slit. The remaining 2 are uncarved. The right-hand corbel of the fifth window from the west has been said to represent Bishop Thomas Kempe (Ill. 5).[89] On the south side the mixture is different. There are only 9 carved heads, 3 lentoid and 6 drilled, one of which may be an animal. Of the rest, one has an angel with an open book, 8 are floral and architectural, and 2 are uncarved. The corbels are set too low in relation to the present height of the windows which leads one to the conclusion that the windows were heightened after 1480, not only to enhance the appearance of the building but also to admit more light into what was to be a room of greater height than before (Ill. 4*b*). The style of the windows does not reflect the taste and delicacy of William Orchard's work, and it is questionable, therefore, whether the change was made by him.

Having considered the floor and the windows of the Library room one must now look at the walls and the roof. During the restoration, and before the internal walls were cleaned, a change of build was clearly visible just above the window heads. The type of stone used at this stage changes from Taynton to Headington where Orchard is known to have owned quarries. It seems likely, therefore, that the height of the walls at this point was to have been that at which the supports for the roof timbers were originally to have been fixed. It

5. A window corbel in Duke Humfrey said to represent Thomas Kempe, Bishop of London. (Thomas-Photos, Oxford)

was necessary, however, to increase the height of the walls, which Orchard duly did, not only to provide additional weight to counter the considerable thrust of the vault below but also to improve the proportions of the room above it. Further weight was added to the walls by the introduction of pinnacles to top them. Now, with higher walls in place, the building was ready to receive the roof. As has been seen, at least one earlier roof had covered part, if not all, of the building, but at a lower level. The present, and final, roof is supported by very tall wall-posts on 12 corbels, 6 on either side. Six of these, originally of fine workmanship, but now somewhat mutilated, one very badly, date from the mid-fifteenth century, before Orchard's time. There must have been a further six of similar date and style, but they have disappeared and were probably irreparably damaged during one or other of the changes of plan. Four were replaced about 1600 and are sketchily carved, another is of rough uncarved stone, and the last, in the north-west corner, is too badly mutilated to be recognisable. However, one must assume that when Orchard came to put the roof on there were twelve corbels set into the walls but at a lower level than was appropriate. Nevertheless, by introducing the tall wall-posts he was able to use them for their original purpose. The rafters were of oak and were visible inside the room. The secondary brackets seen today between the main trusses were not part of the original roof but are seventeenth-century additions.

It is now possible to begin to survey the structure as a whole. The only representation we have of it as a free-standing building is a small sketch by John Bereblock done in 1566 (frontispiece).[90] It is drawn from the north-west and shows the old city wall in the foreground. The windows are shaped rather oddly but the proportions are accurate and the recent discoveries have proved that its detail, in so far as it can be checked, is correct. It shows a porch at the west end and two turrets, one or both of which are known to have contained stone staircases leading to Duke Humfrey's Library. A staircase depicted on the niche containing the bust of Sir Thomas Bodley in the antechapel of Merton College is said to represent one of them (Ill. 6).[91] Remains of the south-west staircase came to light during the restoration. An inner door from the porch led into the Divinity School. The east end is not visible in Bereblock's drawing but there is a central pinnacle on the gable. This was a feature of Orchard's style;

6. Staircase depicted on Sir Thomas Bodley's memorial in Merton College chapel said to represent one of those leading originally to Duke Humfrey's Library.

it occurs also on the west end of the University Church and on Magdalen College antechapel. The doorway into the Divinity School at the east end was as it is today except that it was flanked by two blocked windows of the original design, to which reference has already been made. It was protected, however, as at the west end, by a porch which was removed when the Proscholium was built in 1610. Traces of it came to light in 1968 when the Proscholium was being converted to form the Bodleian main entrance.[92] There was a great east window giving light to the Library and this must have looked very similar to the present window of Arts End, Thomas Bodley's first addition to Duke Humfrey's Library (1610–12). It is likely that he deliberately set out to copy fairly closely the window which had to be removed to make way for his extension. In a letter to his Librarian, Thomas James, dated 27 January 1612, he asked for information about the size of it.[93] Flanking the east window on the outside of the building were at least two decorative niches with stone canopies. These were first revealed in 1898 during the course of work on the floor of Arts End but they were not then studied in detail.[94] The more recent renovation of the same floor has shown that their characteristics

7 (a) (b) (c). Carved heads revealed on the east façade of the building during restoration work, and the niche which concealed one of them. (Thomas-Photos, Oxford)

(a)

(b)

(*c*)

compare exactly with those of similar niches associated with the
Divinity School vault, and therefore they must have been part of
Orchard's design. Careful photography has revealed two heads
carved on bosses inside the canopies, a male and a female, which must
have been totally invisible if, as is likely, statues were placed in the
niches (Ill. 7). The date when the niches were constructed was
probably about 1481 because half-way through that year Bishop
Kempe was urged by the University to inspect the work for which he
had provided the money. He was told that the workmen were as busy
as bees, some carrying stones, some polishing them, others carving
the statues and placing them in their niches.[95] The façades at both
ends of the building were originally stone-panelled and this feature
was copied by Bodley when he built Arts End. Some of the original
panelling may still be seen inside the Proscholium. A conjectural
drawing of the eastern façade as it would have looked in 1488 was

8. Suggested appearance of the east façade of the building in 1488. (Drawing by Robert Potter)

made by Robert Potter, based upon discoveries made during the restoration work of the 1960s, of which he was the architect (Ill. 8).

The very protracted period of building, 65 years in all, was now almost at an end. The Divinity School may possibly have been in use from about 1467, after the desks had been made, but it must have been out of commission while the vault was being inserted (1480–3). The library room above cannot have been in use at all until 1488. In 1487 the University had received information from a source of unimpeachable veracity that Bishop Kempe was going to make a donation of books. They hastened to assure him that the books would be chained in his new library as soon as it was ready to receive them.[96] In the following year an unidentified member of the University, having given a number of volumes, was informed that they had been chained, as he had requested, and that they constituted the first donation received for the new library.[97]

No mention can be found of desks or any other fittings for the

9. Silhouettes of the original lecterns in Duke Humfrey's Library. (Thomas-Photos, Oxford)

10. Suggested appearance of the interior of the Library in 1488. (Drawing by Robert Potter)

library. It might have been expected that the desks from Bishop Cobham's library, to which the manuscripts were chained, and the seats which accompanied them, would be transferred but this was not so. In 1489 John Russell, Bishop of Lincoln and Chancellor of the University, suggested that they should be moved to the new School of Canon Law when finished,[98] to which the University replied that when the time came to take a decision about their future nothing would be done contrary to his wishes.[99] Lecterns were, however, provided for the new library and the restoration has revealed the silhouettes, on the walls between the windows, of their pointed ends, the height of which was about 5 ft. 6 in. and related to a floor at much the same level as it is today (Ill. 9). These discoveries, and others already mentioned, enabled Mr Potter to make a drawing of the likely appearance of the interior of Duke Humfrey's Library in 1488 (Ill. 10) when it was opened to readers for the first time.

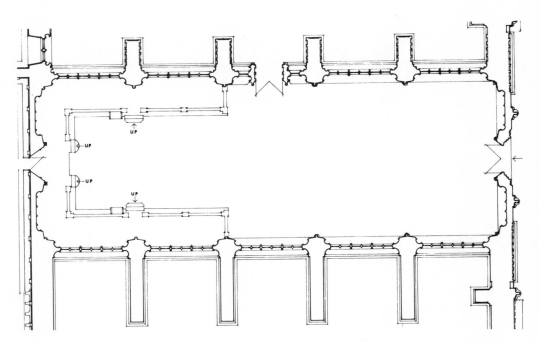

FIGURE 1. The Divinity School

II

The Interior Decoration of the Divinity School

THE Divinity School is a simple rectangle measuring about 87 feet from east to west and 31 feet from north to south. It consists of five bays each lighted by a window on each side. Nine of the windows consist of six lights with tracery above, but the tenth, the central window on the north side, was altered in 1669 to accommodate a doorway. They were originally embellished with shields-of-arms of benefactors and others but none of this stained glass now remains. Some of it, according to Anthony Wood, was destroyed by Edward VI's Commissioners but not all can have met this fate because Richard Lee, when he made his visitation of Oxfordshire in 1574, was able to make sketches in his notebook of 33 shields 'in glasse' in the School. He attempted identifications of only four of them, however, and did not indicate on which wall they were to be found.[1] Another collection of sketches of the shields was made by Sir William Dugdale in about 1645. He began at the west end of the north side and drew 32 shields in all, 21 on the north side and 11 on the south, but did not attempt to name them.[2] Anthony Wood produced 24 drawings of the shields as they were in 1658[3] and, at about the same time, Nathaniel Greenwood, a friend of his, included in his notes on the stained glass in college chapels and halls and in Oxfordshire churches a list of that in the School, giving the heraldic descriptions.[4] Neither indicated the positions of the shields or attempted to identify them. The list which Wood included in the manuscript of his History of the University, compiled between 1674 and 1685, followed closely the sketches of Dugdale.[5] He headed it 'Arms in the windows' but one cannot be sure that the stained glass was actually in place at the time at which he was writing. It is possible that it was all removed when the north door was constructed in 1669. He gave the heraldic descriptions but named only a few of them. When John Gutch edited and published the manuscript in 1792–6 he emended the heading to read 'Arms [that were] in the windows' and added identifications to most of them.[6] A comparison of the shields once in the windows with those on the vault reveals the fact that almost all of those on the north side were repeated on the vault whereas the reverse is the case on the south.

The east and west walls of the School, containing the original doorways, have panelled compartments and are decorated with fifteenth-century images. Over the doorway at the east end was originally the Rood. This no longer exists but the images remain: Our Lady and St John on either side with St Peter (headless) and St Paul below. It is not known when St Peter lost his head but he is depicted without it in a drawing by John Buckler in 1804.[7] Figures are housed also in the moulding of the arch above representing angels, disputing doctors, a bishop, and an archbishop. At the west end the figures represent Our Lady showing an open book to the infant Christ, and the four Evangelists, with figures in the moulding similar to those at the east end. It is, however, the English Gothic stone-vaulted roof of the utmost complexity which is the crowning glory of this magnificent room, probably the largest groined vault of one span in any secular building in this country. Its elaborate decoration is computed to contain no fewer than 455 bosses, 91 in each bay,[8] bearing shields-of-arms, initials, words and sentences in English, French and Latin, religious subjects such as the Madonna and Child (Ill. 11), the Holy Trinity (Ill. 12) and St. Veronica, together with representations of animals, fruit, foliage, and the like. Many of the ribs of the vault terminate in pendants, four in each bay, which have canopied housings for images on each face (Ill. 13a–b). The five bays are identical in layout. As with the shields in the windows the earliest extant sketches of those on the vault were made by Richard Lee (1574) who produced forty-one but attempted names to only two.[9] Next are Anthony Wood's drawings of 1658, forty-three in all, some of which are named.[10] Then follows the list in his History of the University which was expanded when John Gutch published it.[11] At least two partial lists of early nineteenth-century date exist in manuscript in the Bodleian and in 1887 Herbert Hurst drafted a description of the vault together with a complete list of all the various decorative features.[12] The first detailed study of the vault to be printed appeared in 1914 from the pen of W. H. St John Hope.[13] Unfortunately it is marred by the fact that the details of the decoration on the north and south ends of the second and third bays from the west have become transposed. This error was corrected by

11. Divinity School vault. The Madonna and Child. Third bay from the west, north end, central key. (Thomas-Photos, Oxford)

12. Divinity School vault. The Trinity. Third bay from the west, south end, central key. (Thomas-Photos, Oxford)

H. Edith Legge who produced a useful guide for visitors in 1923.[14] In 1939 a selective list appeared in the Oxford volume of the Royal Commission on Historical Monuments.[15] The late E. A. Greening Lamborn, an Oxford headmaster whose knowledge of heraldry was extensive, was somewhat critical of the standard of accuracy of some of the descriptions of the bosses and was able to make suggestions for corrections at proof stage.[16] Later, in the pages of *Notes and Queries*, he offered further identifications of shields hitherto unnamed. He also made the comment 'The men who cut the shields were masons, not heralds, and it was inevitable that among such a large collection of coats there should be an occasional failure to copy exactly the drawing supplied to the carver. For the most part this does not prevent us from recognising what was intended.'[17] In 1913, when the bosses and carvings were dusted and cleaned, a small syndicate of senior members of the University commissioned F. H. Crossley to make a detailed photographic record of them,[18] a copy of which was presented to the Bodleian in 1914. It is indexed on the basis of the descriptions of St John Hope.[19]

From evidence derived from the decoration it is safe to assume that the vault was built between 1480 and 1483 and that work began at the west end.[20] Moreover, the number of bosses bearing arms or other personal details becomes smaller as one progresses from west to east, perhaps indicating a growing shortage of people worthy of com-

13. Divinity School vault. Two pendants; (*a*) St Mark with lion and book, (*b*) a pope. (Thomas-Photos, Oxford)

memoration. Two interesting questions arise from a study of the names of those selected for that honour—who was responsible for choosing them, and on what basis were they chosen? Chancellors of the University took a more active part in the administration than they do today and it is likely the Chancellor in office from 1479 until 1484, Lionel Wydville (Ill. 14), would have been involved in the deliberations, together with one or more of the Vice-Chancellors, the Proctors, and members of Congregation. Unfortunately the register of that body covering the relevant period has not survived. Most of the names represented on the vault fall into distinct categories of persons whom one might expect to find there, but there are a few (if the shields have been correctly identified) whose connection with the University or the School is not clear. The largest group consists of Chancellors of the University dating almost from the commencement of the building. Other University officials—the High Steward, Vice-Chancellors (Commissaries), and Proctors—to whom tribute is paid held office only towards the end of the building period. Archbishops of Canterbury, with one exception, are commemorated, like the

[34]

Chancellors, from early days but those of York are not so honoured (Ills. 15, 16). A number of bishops, particularly of Lincoln, are represented, some as benefactors (Ill. 17), others by virtue of being Chancellors of the University. In general terms an order of importance is noticeable; archbishops, bishops, chancellors, and benefactors merited a shield, some with initials in addition; others had to be content with names or initials and most of this group were living at the time of construction of the vault.

For a detailed description of the decoration of the vault the reader should turn to the authorities already mentioned (Hope, Legge, and RCHM), for it would not be possible or appropriate to repeat their work here: but a few points are worthy of particular comment. The

14. Divinity School vault. Central section of the westernmost bay. The shield of arms of Lionel Wydville in the centre and the adjacent shields are mutilated by the holes through which formerly hung the supports for the canopy over the Regius Professor's high chair. (Thomas-Photos, Oxford)

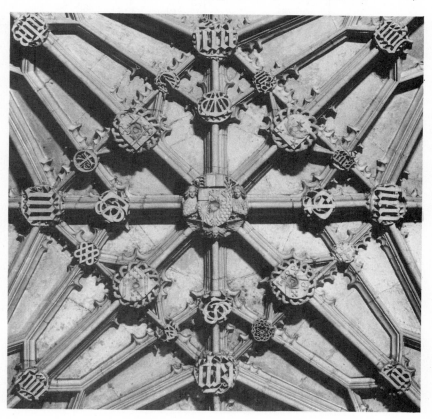

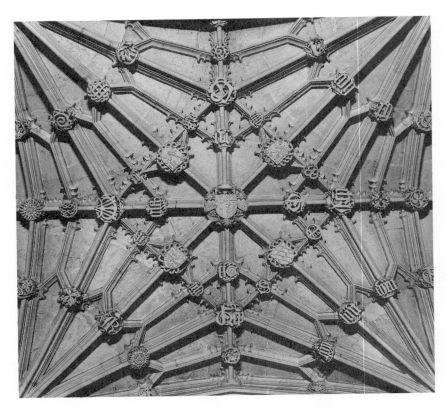

15. Divinity School vault. Central section of the second bay from the west. In the centre is the shield of arms of Thomas Bourchier, Cardinal Archbishop of Canterbury 1454–86 and Chancellor of the University 1433–7. (Thomas-Photos, Oxford

royal arms of King Edward IV, who died in 1483, the year in which the vault was completed, occupy the central key of the central bay (Ill. 18). He visited Oxford in 1481 and must have seen the vault in course of construction. On Monday 24 September he

was pleased to be present at public Disputations, and to hear his Divinity Lecture (lately erected by him in the University) read by Lionell Wydevill the Chancellor: to the hearing of which, he about this time had sent his Nephew Edm. Poole (whom the University in their letters do highly commend) and other young men of his blood. After the King had visited several parts of the University and heard scholastical exercises he departed with great content.[21]

Neither Duke Humfrey nor Cardinal Beaufort is commemorated on the vault, but the shields of both are reputed to have been in the

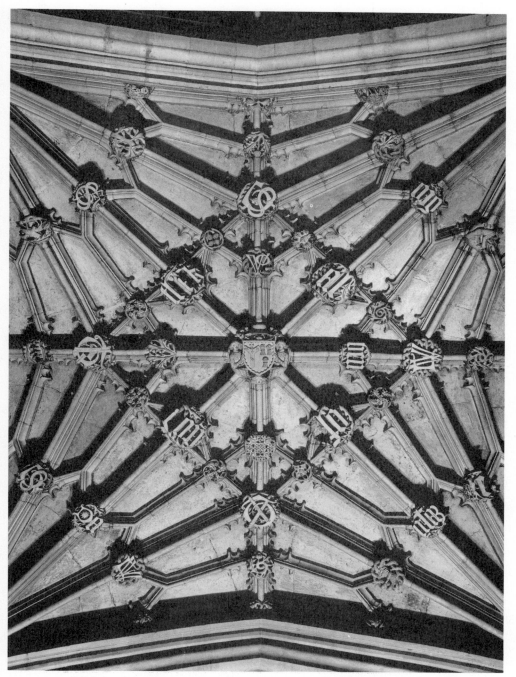

16. Divinity School vault. Central section of the fourth bay from the west. In the centre is the shield of arms of John Kempe, Cardinal Archbishop of Canterbury 1452–4. (Thomas-Photos, Oxford)

17. Divinity School vault. North section of the
middle bay. The crossed swords of the bishopric
of London impaling the three sheaves of Kempe.
The left-hand boss, which has been cut away to
admit Thomas Kempe's shield, represents the
rayed rose of King Edward IV. (Thomas-Photos,
Oxford)

stained glass on the south side and the arms carved in stone on the
cornice on the outside of the north wall are believed to represent the
former.[22]

Most of the shields on the vault have been identified although there
are divergencies of opinion upon a few. Attempts have also been
made to fit names to the initials which appear there, and to discover
the relevance of some of the words. Upon closer investigation a
pattern emerges which has not hitherto been remarked upon. The
arms of the University of Oxford appear on the vault in six places;
but of individual colleges, only one is honoured in this way. The
Exeter College shield occurs three times. The college was, and is, the
Divinity School's closest neighbour, a relationship which cannot
always have been an easy one during the exceptionally long building
period when noise and other disturbances must have caused great
inconvenience. Its representation on the ceiling of the completed
School was, therefore, perhaps a token of the University's gratitude
for many years of patient forbearance. This consideration apart,
however, there seems to have been a college influence on the choice
of some of the names and initials which appear there in addition to the
shields. The Vice-Chancellor from 1470 to 1479 was an Exeter man,

[38]

Thomas Stevyn, DD. He may well have been involved in the selection of names to be commemorated, and the initials T.S. with a doctor's cap over, in the middle section of the westernmost bay, probably refer to him. A look at the names of graduates of the college about 1480–3 makes it possible to suggest solutions to some of the other words and initials which hitherto have not been identified, and alternatives to existing attributions. Again, in the middle section of the westernmost bay, are two words 'Row' and 'Ruer' whose meaning has not previously been hazarded. Hope thought they might form part of a sentence in French.[23] It is now suggested that they refer to two graduates of the college. John Rowe was admitted in 1475 and was a Fellow until 1490. Thomas Ruer was admitted in 1479, already a graduate, and was a Fellow until 1491. He was Rector of the college in 1487–8. In the same section of the vault two further bosses may relate to Exeter men. The name 'Orell' appears there (and also in the next bay). This has previously been thought to be a tribute to William Orell who was Proctor in 1439, the year in which Duke Humfrey made his first large gift of books. In the light of the fact that most of the names and initials on the vault appear to be those of persons living at the time of its construction it seems more likely that John Orell was the honorand. He was Senior Fellow of the college in 1478 and Rector in 1478–9. Also in the same bay are

18. Divinity School vault. In the centre. The royal arms of King Edward IV. (Thomas-Photos, Oxford)

the initials W.C. If they have a college connection they could refer to Walter Coose who was Chaplain in 1478 and a Fellow for a further ten years. In the second bay from the west there are four bosses whose lettering together has been conjectured to form the name Will Merefeld, but the college connection has not previously been mentioned. He was a B.A. on admission in 1475 and became Rector in 1479–80. Two further suggestions are offered. The initials I.B. occur twice in the easternmost bay. The only previous guess at the identity has been made in RCHM where John Bettys, Proctor in 1476, is mentioned as a possible candidate. Appearing, as they do, in the last bay to be completed, in 1483, the initials are more likely to be those of another Exeter College man, James Babbe, who was Senior Proctor in that year and Rector in 1482–3. Babbe, Merefeld, and a third member of the college, John Mayne, used an Exeter College book, which is now in the Bodleian, as a caution for a loan in 1479.[24] Mayne was a Fellow from 1477 until about 1489 and was in holy orders. On the same section of the vault as Merefeld is the monogram J.M.V. which has not so far been identified. It is tempting to think that it might refer to Mayne.

III

The Divinity School after 1488

THE year 1488, therefore, was notable for the completion of a University building in the heart of Oxford, containing two splendid rooms, very different in design and decoration, one for the teaching of theology, the subject of the greatest prestige in medieval universities, the other for housing the University Library. Although the latter was not ready to receive the books until 1488 it is reasonable to suppose that the School, which had been in use for some years before its vaulted ceiling was put in place, was again available for teaching purposes as soon as the vault had been completed. Candidates for the degrees of Bachelor and Doctor of Divinity performed their 'exercises' in the School and Regius Professors of Divinity delivered their lectures therein.[1] Appropriate furniture, suitably arranged, was required for the proper performance of these rites. The examination proceedings were conducted by a moderator who occupied a raised seat, used also by the Regius Professor, and the candidate had to respond to questions put to him by an opponent. The two disputants faced each other from lower positions and the audience occupied the eastern part of the room. The disputations were originally formidable intellectual exercises and many candidates failed to pass the test, but in the course of time the standard gradually fell until, by the end of the eighteenth century, no intellectual effort at all was required and prearranged questions met with prearranged answers. Eventually disputations were abolished and written examinations took their place. These continued to be conducted in the School until the opening of the new Examination Schools in High Street in 1882.[2]

Upon completion of the vault, therefore, it is likely that the thirty-seven desks and seats, purchased in 1466, would have been put back in place. In addition some carved fittings, including a professor's chair (*cathedra*), were installed before 1489 because reference was made to them in an undated letter to Bishop Kempe, who died in that year.[3] According to Anthony Wood, writing about alterations to the School carried out in 1669, 'before that time all the ancient seats with desks before them on each side of the School from one end to the other were taken away.'[4] He has also left a description of the ceremonial seats which were in the School before 1669.[5] The Regius Professor of Divinity's chair stood in the middle of the School on the south side. It was a 'fair piece of polisht work' erected on stone pillars surmounted by a canopy of carved wood supported by stone pillars and reaching almost to the ceiling. The opponent's seat was under it 'on the stone work of which were the arms of Moreton Archbishop of Canterbury and Cardinal, as if he had been the builder of, or a benefactor to, it'. The respondent's seat was opposite, on the north side of the School, 'built also of polisht stone, erected from the floor, and half encompassed with a stone seat for the auditors'. John Moreton was Archbishop of Canterbury from 1486 until his death in 1500 and Chancellor of the University from 1494. His arms, according to Wood's list, appeared also in one of the windows on the south side of the School. Wood tells us that the Professor's seat was dismantled in 1669, which may mean that it was retained for use again in a different position, but the other two seats were removed entirely. We do not know, however, how much, if any, of the original furniture survived the visitation of Edward VI's commissioners in 1550.

It was primarily Duke Humfrey's Library against which the Edwardian visitors directed their energies but the Divinity School did not escape entirely, and the building as a whole deteriorated as time went by. Anthony Wood describes the plight of the School:

It suffered in its roof and gutters of lead, which being not repaired for several years, great damage followed thereupon. Part of its useful furniture was taken away by Mechanics, and the windows that were adorned with the pictures of some saints and fathers as also with the arms of benefactors were partly broken and the lead belonging to them and any thing else that could be easily pilfered, were quite taken away. Also not only nettles, bushes, and brambles grew around the walls . . . but a stinking pound for cattle were erected close, and joining to it. All which being beheld with great reluctancy by the R. Catholics when their religion was restored, were taken away and all things relating to the School were put into good order, an. 1557.'[6]

The accession of the Catholic Queen Mary having taken place in 1553 the restoration of the Divinity School may have been put in hand before 1557. It was certainly in use in April 1554 when Archbishop Cranmer was taken there to enter into a disputation concerning the presence of Christ in the Eucharist[7] and again on 30 September in the following year when the Commissioners appointed to examine Ridley and Latimer 'took their place upon the high seat made for disputations and lectures, which was set fairly forth with cloth of tissue and cushions of velvet'.[8]

Three structural alterations were made to the School in the ensuing years. The first was in 1610 when Sir Thomas Bodley began to build his first extension to the Library above, involving the construction of the Proscholium and the removal of the porch over the eastern door of the School to make way for it. The second, in 1634, when the Convocation House and library room over it (Selden End) were built, necessitated the removal of the western porch and the two staircase turrets leading to Duke Humfrey's Library. Neither of these alterations affected the appearance of the interior of the School but the third, in 1669, regrettably spoilt the symmetry of the north side. It is forcefully described by an eminent student of seventeenth-century Oxford, writing in 1906

The central window has been shamefully marred by thrusting a doorway into it. This was done . . . to allow the procession of Vice-Chancellor, Doctors and Proctors, to be formed in the Divinity School for great academical functions, thence to pass, by a short and straight course, into the Sheldonian opposite. The great name of Christopher Wren, the designer of the doorway, is no excuse for the vandalism of unnecessarily destroying a beautiful window and, with it, the whole side of the finest building in Oxford.[9]

The doorway has a small stone porch, in the ceiling of which is carved an open book bearing, in Greek, words from St Luke 2:46: 'They found him sitting in the midst of the doctors.' In front, on the canopy, is the monogram CWA which may stand for Christopher Wren, Architect. Over the window containing the doorway is an early eighteenth-century cartouche containing the University arms.

The Vice-Chancellor's Computus for 1668–9 gives an account of the cost of inserting the north door and of other work on the Divinity School and round about it:

to Mr. Bird for the worke done in securing the vault of the Divinity Schole, making the new dore, altering the professor's seat and the windowes, making a large sewer from the south side of the library round about the Convocation house into the sewer &c. 101 li.; to Richard Frogley the carpenter for scaffolding within and without the Divinity Schole, and for worke done in newe laying the gutters over it, as also for worke about the printing house, 38 li. 15s 11d; to Young the smith for cramps for the vault for the Divinity Schole, and for the iron worke of the type over the professor's chair, 40 li.; to Bernard Rawlins for glazing work in all the Scholes and lead and work for the new pipes and for cramps in and about the Divinity Schole, 107 li. 13s 9d; to Mr. Cleer, London, joyner, in part, for work done by him and his brother the carver, in the Divinity Schole, 147 li.

In the Computus for 1669–70 we find further payments: 'to Mr. Hawkins for painting in the Divinity Schole, 19 li. 12s; to Clere the joyner for worke in the Divinity Schole, 60 li.; to Edmund Smith for worke in the Divinity Schole, 11 li. 9s'.[10]

With the exception of the brothers William and Richard Cleer, who were Londoners, and possibly Edmund Smith about whom nothing seems to be known, the craftsmen were all Oxonians. William Byrd,[11] stone-carver, who discovered a method of painting or staining marble was, with the Cleers and Richard Frogley, currently working for Christopher Wren on the Sheldonian Theatre (1664–69).[12] In addition to making the new north doorway facing the Theatre Byrd was called upon to strengthen the vault in which some defects must have been found and for which the iron cramps were made by William Young, the smith, and to alter the Professor's seat which, as described above, was supported on stone pillars and, according to Wood, had been dismantled. The brothers Cleer were paid over £200 for joinery, a considerable sum, which must have been mainly for the raised platforms and seats at the west end of the School. There is no record of the painting for which Richard Hawkins was paid £19 12s. 0d. He was a prominent Oxford citizen (d. 1699), an alderman, and mayor in 1689–90. His skills seem to have been in the field of decorative and heraldic painting, rather than in ordinary house-painting, and he had a knowledge of coats of arms.[13] He, together with Richard Frogley, carpenter, William Young, smith, and Bernard Rawlins, glazier, was still at work ten years later, in the (Old) Ashmolean Museum (1679–83).[14]

The state of the vault during the ensuing centuries, until 1960, was

at times precarious and its vicissitudes are described below in relation
to the condition of the library floor above it, but Wren's iron cramps
of 1669 do not appear to have had the desired effect of adding
strength to the structure. In 1700, when he was called in again, the
workmen reported that the four main arches of the vault were
cracked on the south side a little above the position of the 'cramps and
bolts' (see p. 67 below). In 1877, when Douglas Galton supervised
repairs to the building (see p. 72 below) he found that the vault
required only slight attention but reported that there was one
blemish, namely, 'the old iron fastenings near the springings of the
main ribs, which are of little if any service in strengthening the vault'.
Some correction of settlement, some rejointing, and general cleaning
of the masonry was carried out at the end of the major structural
reinforcement of the whole building which took place in the early
1960s under the auspices of the Oxford Historic Buildings Fund. In
their report on the work of the Fund, *Oxford Stone Restored*, ed.
Oakeshott (1975), the Trustees recorded that 'It was decided to leave
in position the nineteenth-century iron ties piercing the masonry
arches for fear of causing greater damage to the moulded work by
their removal: it did not appear that excessive corrosion of the metal
was taking place.' These 'nineteenth-century' iron ties are secured to
the four principal arches on both sides of the building, each by six
large bolts. In the light of the reference of 1700 to 'cramps and bolts'
and to that of Galton in 1877 to 'old iron fastenings' it would seem
likely that the ties are, in fact, those introduced by Wren in 1669.

The earliest engraving of the inside of the School was published by
David Loggan in 1675, soon after the alterations had been completed
(Ill. 19). It shows the Professor's seat on high at the west end,
supported on pillars with a canopy over, the fixing holes for which
may still be seen in the vault. It would appear to correspond fairly
closely with Wood's description of it in earlier times. The wooden
pulpits for the opponent and respondent face each other from the
north and south sides. A wooden balustrade divides the two western
bays from the rest of the room but with a gap in the centre which
could be closed by wooden gates. Further changes took place in the
nineteenth century. The Professor's high chair, the canopy and the
balustrade were still in position in 1842 (Ill. 20) and remained for at
least another thirty years for they appear in a photograph of about
1872 (see p. 86 n. 2). Alterations, however, took place within the

[45]

Interior Prospectus SCHOLÆ THEO LOGICÆ OXONÍJ quam An.º 1427. Academiæ Sumptibus inchoatam absolvit Humphredus Dux Glocestriæ

Venerabili Eruditissimoq; Viro, Dº Richardo Allestry, Sctæ Theologiæ apud Oxoni- sis Præposito, Typum hunc Scholæ Theologicæ Alioru Arte et Munificentia or

The inside of the DIVINITIE SCHOOLE in Oxford begun by the Vniuersity A°. 1427. and afterward finished by Humphrey Duke of Glocester.

Dav. Loggan delin. et sculp. cum Privil. S.R.M.

enses Professori Regio, Ædis Christi ibidem Canonico, et Collegij Regalis Etonen-natissimis at Ipsius Doctrina & Acumine impensius decoratæ. D.D.C.Q. Dav. Loggan.

19. The interior of the Divinity School. (From D. Loggan, *Oxonia Illustrata,* 1675)

20. Exercise for the Degree of Bachelor of Divinity, 1842. The Regius Professor in the pulpit is Renn Dickson Hampden, DD, afterwards Bishop of Hereford. His appointment to the Chair, and later to the bishopric both met with opposition on account of his unorthodox views. (G.A. Oxon. a. 72, p. 77)

next decade and the high chair and the canopy were removed. The two side pulpits survived but had been lowered by 1900. The wood-work at the west end today is of seventeenth-century origin and there is little doubt that it is basically part of that which was introduced in 1669.[15]

The Faculty of Theology has not been the only occupant of the School over the years. Eminent deceased persons have lain in state, kings and princes have peered at the ceiling; the House of Commons, driven from London by the plague, met there in 1625; the Assizes have taken place there; senior academics have donned their robes and ceremonial processions have been marshalled therein. The most elaborate arrangements were made to receive the body of William Juxon, Archbishop of Canterbury, once President of St John's College, who died on 4 June 1663 and was to be interred in the college chapel on 9 July. The west end of the School was practically cleared of furniture, the floor was raised six inches, and an additional raised platform constructed on which the coffin was to rest. The cortège was due to arrive on the afternoon of Tuesday 7 July but as it reached the Oxford side of Wheatley a tremendous storm broke which flooded the streets of the city and held up the proceedings for an hour and a half. However, the coffin was eventually put in place, draped in velvet hangings, with streamers bearing the archbishop's coat of arms, his mitre on a velvet cushion at the head and candles in silver candlesticks strategically placed. On the following day the spectacle was open to the public. Finally on the Thursday the body was laid to rest in St John's.[16] Twenty years later Sir Leoline Jenkins, a generous benefactor to Jesus College, lay in state guarded by four undergraduates from the College before interment in the chapel on 17 September 1685.[17] One further lying-in-state must be mentioned, that of Dr John Radcliffe in 1714, before burial in the University Church. The body was conveyed to the great gate of the Schools Quadrangle from whence 'it was carried upon Men's Shoulders to the Divinity School, & there placed, the School being hung in Mourning . . . & everything adapted as to Scutcheons, Lights &c. that is proper to so solemn an Occasion.'[18]

Throughout the centuries royal visitors have been attracted to Oxford and many have viewed the Divinity School. One example must suffice. King Charles II in 1681 went incognito to the School where he was received by the Vice-Chancellor, Timothy Halton, Provost of Queen's, the Bishop of Oxford, John Fell, and Sir Leoline Jenkins, and 'spent some time in viewing the roofe thereof, so much admired by forreigners for its great varietie of exquisit sculpture'.[19] In 1752, when Oxford Town Hall was being rebuilt, the Assizes were held in the School, the University having refused the use of the Sheldonian Theatre. Mary Blandy was due to be tried on 3 March for the murder of her father but 'owing to the insertion overnight by a mischievous undergraduate or other sympathiser with the day's heroine of some obstacle in the keyhole, the door could not be opened, and the lock had to be forced, which delayed the proceedings for an hour.' The judges returned to their lodgings and the trial eventually began at eight o'clock. It went on for thirteen hours.[20]

In the nineteenth century, the Bodleian Library, thirsting for additional space, began to cast longing glances at the Divinity School. In 1856 Sir Gilbert Scott suggested that it would make a splendid daytime reading room, 'a use to which, both from its great amount of light and its architectural beauty, it seems pre-eminently fitted'. Had anything come of it, he would have proposed the introduction of decorative glass, and of colour on the walls and vault.[21] In 1878 the suggestion was renewed and it was estimated that space could be found for a hundred readers. This reached the stage of a draft statute but it was never put before Congregation.[22] In 1882 the newly-appointed Librarian, E. W. B. Nicholson, thought that the School would make a reading-room suitable for the consultation of periodicals but it is difficult to imagine how sufficient shelving and desks could have been introduced into the room without depriving it of most of its natural light and without debasing it utterly.[23] On 5 February 1929 Congregation granted the use of the School to the Bodleian Curators for exhibitions for a period not exceeding five years at such times as it was not required for University purposes. Four show-cases were commissioned at a cost of £200 but the arrangement did not last very long. For reasons of economy the Curators discontinued it in Hilary Term 1932.[24] Almost forty more years were to elapse before the Divinity School officially, and appropriately, became part of the Bodleian Library, the nucleus of which it had supported, through good times and bad, for nearly five centuries. Together with the Convocation House at its west end it was transferred to the care of the Bodleian Curators in March 1968 and now forms one of the Library's exhibition rooms.[25]

IV

Duke Humfrey's Library
after 1488

FROM 1488 until 1550 there is an almost total lack of historical information about Duke Humfrey's Library. The post of University Librarian had, from 1412, when an elaborate body of Library statutes was drawn up, been combined with that of University Chaplain and the names of some of the holders of the office are recorded:[1]

In 1449 John Fytzjamys. Apparently not MA.
In 1457–62? Stephen Tyler, MA. Principal of Beam Hall.
?–1506 John Foster, or Forster, MA. Fellow of Merton College.
1506–13 John Wayte, MA. Fellow of Merton College.
1513–20? Adam Byrkebeke, MA. Fellow of Queen's College.
1520?–21 William Smythe, MA. Rector of Exeter College.
1521–41? Edmund Fletcher, MA. Fellow of Exeter College and Rector in 1526–9.
1541?–43 Whytt (White), MA. Possibly Richard White, secular chaplain, MA. 1532. Not identified in Emden.
1543–53? Humfry Burneford, MA. Fellow of Merton College.

There seems to have been a lack of concern for the safety of the books. Borrowing in return for pledges was permitted but some were paltry in relation to the value of the books borrowed and some of the borrowers were prepared to forfeit the pledge rather than return the book.[2] Mutilation of books must also have been a problem, for Humfry Blewett of Merton College was, in 1528, permitted to borrow a book of astronomical tables in order to restore a portion which had been cut out.[3] There is no evidence of any provision for the acquisition of new books, either manuscript or printed. It is likely that little money was available for the upkeep of the Library and it was Thomas Bodley's view that the lack of endowment was partly responsible for the fate which befell it in 1550.[4]

King Edward VI's visitation of Oxford University began in 1549, and in the following year his Visitors, prominent among them

Richard Cox, Dean of Christ Church and later Bishop of Ely, directed their attention to the treasures of Oxford. Painted windows were removed, at least one college reredos was smashed, anything considered to be popish was condemned, college libraries and the University Library itself were pillaged.[5] In Anthony Wood's words Dean Cox 'shewed himself so zealous in purging this place of its rarities, especially such that had Rubrics in them or any way savoured (as he thought) of superstition, that he left not one of those goodly MSS.' He went on to say that 'some of those books so taken out by the Reformers were burnt, some sold away for Robin Hood's pennyworths, either to Booksellers, or to Glovers to press their gloves, or Taylors to make measures, or to Bookbinders to cover books bound by them, and some also kept by the Reformers for their own use.'[6] Six years later nothing was left of Duke Humfrey's Library except the totally bare room for, by a decree in Convocation of 25 January 1555/6, the desks and seats were sold, probably to Christ Church.[7] The room itself was later handed over to the Faculty of Medicine whose students had formerly used the Divinity School for their lectures.[8]

In 1560, only ten years after the desecration of Duke Humfrey's Library, Thomas Bodley entered Magdalen College, Oxford as an undergraduate at the age of fifteen. After graduating in 1563 he moved to Merton College, becoming a Fellow in the following year. Having taken his Master of Arts degree in 1567 he served as Proctor in 1569, his companion in office being John Bereblock of Exeter College whose drawing of the Divinity School and Duke Humfrey's Library (1566) is the earliest in existence. Bodley, however, was not content to spend the rest of his life as an academic. In 1576 he set out on his travels to Europe in the course of which he became proficient in Italian, French and Spanish. After four years he returned to England and after several attempts succeeded in becoming a member of Parliament. In 1585 and for the next ten years he carried out a number of diplomatic missions abroad during which time he wooed a rich west-country widow, Ann Ball, and married her only four months after her first husband's death. Nicholas Ball's fortune had been amassed from trading in pilchards and it is no secret that it was this money which enabled Bodley to restore and endow the Library which now bears his name.

After his recall from Holland in 1596, Bodley did not return to the

Continent again. In his autobiography he relates that, after much thought, he considered that he possessed four attributes necessary to enable him to undertake a project which would occupy him for the rest of his life, knowledge, money, friends, and leisure. In his own, oft-quoted, words:

I concluded at the last to set vp my Staffe at the Librarie dore in Oxon; being throwghly perswaded, that in my solitude, and surcease from the Commonwealth affayers, I coulde not busie my selfe to better purpose, then by redusing that place (which then in euery part laye ruined and wast) to the publique vse of Studients.[9]

The offer to restore the former University Library (Duke Humfrey's name was never mentioned in any of Bodley's letters) was made to the Vice-Chancellor on 23 February 1597/8:

Where there hath bin heretofore a publike library in Oxford: which you know is apparant, by the rome it self remayning, and by your statute records I will take the charge and cost vpon me, to reduce it again to his former vse: and to make it fitte, and handsome with seates, and shelfes, and Deskes, and all that may be needfull, to stirre vp other mens benevolence, to helpe to furnish it with bookes. And this I purpose to beginne, assoone as timber can be gotten, to the intent that you may reape, some spedie profitt of my proiect.[10]

Having received the blessing of the University Bodley lost no time in getting to work. He wrote again to the Vice-Chancellor on 19 March 1597/8 asking that a committee be set up to consider 'the fittest kinde of facture of deskes, and other furniture'. He proposed to visit Oxford before Easter and to bring with him the sketch of a plan which had been prepared with the help of Sir Henry Savile, Warden of Merton. This was probably a plan of the bookcases based upon those recently constructed in Merton College 'so that . . . we shall soone resolve vpon the best, aswell for shewe, and statly forme, as for capacitie and strength and commoditie of Students'. He had also been offered some timber, albeit unseasoned, by Merton College, but he was loth to use it too quickly 'least by making to muche hast, if the shelfes and seates should chance to warpe, it might proue to be an eyesoare'.[11] Bodley mentions only shelving and seats but wood must also have been required for repairs to the roof. It is known that the latter was in a bad state because Sir Dudley Carleton, in a letter of

3 April 1599 to John Chamberlain, said 'Bodley is looked for daily at Oxford: his library costs him much more than he expected, because the timber works of the house were rotten and had to be new made.'[12] The University, however, took some responsibility for roof repairs because their accounts show an expenditure of £54 10s. 2½d. on it in the years 1597–9.[13] Nowhere in Bodley's letters, however, is there any specific mention of the painted ceiling, but it has always been assumed that he was responsible for it. The square panels contain the arms of the University and at the intersections of the ribs are shields with Bodley's arms upon them. A number of the panels have been renewed over the years but the woodwork is basically seventeenth-century as is the scrollwork on the main timbers.[14] At the end of 1599 Bodley wrote to his Librarian, Thomas James 'Within this fortnight, I trust, I shall haue ended with my carpenters, ioiners, caruers, glasiers, and all that idle rabble: and then I goe in hand, with making vp my barres, lockes, haspes, grates, cheines, and other gimmoes of iron, belonging to the fastning and riuetting of the bookes.'[15] Six months later he was able to inform the Vice-Chancellor that he had 'brought to some good passe the mechanicall workes apperteyning to the Library' and that he had begun 'to busy my selfe, and my frendes, about gathering in Bookes of such as will bee benefactours'.[16]

Bodley was not yet ready, however, to open the restored Library to readers. He wished to wait until its shelves were well-stocked and would create a good impression. At length he was satisfied and the formal opening ceremony took place on 8 November 1602. Bodley himself was not present. The storage space for books was limited. The folios were housed in the large cases projecting at right angles from the walls of the room, as they are today, with three rows of shelving on either side of each case. The counters were about five inches broader than they are now and all in one piece. They could be raised up and secured by a hook fastened on the side of the case above. The alcoves between the cases were provided with benches so that the readers could sit and consult the books which were chained to the shelves in front of them, printed and manuscript in one sequence. There were at first no shelves beneath the counters but some had been inserted by about 1605 as a temporary measure. Attached to the end of each case was a frame, divided in the centre by a vertical partition, containing lists of the books on either side of the case. The books, shelved with their foredges outwards, were arranged by the four faculties—Theology, Law, Medicine, and Arts. The exact location of each faculty at this time cannot be stated with certainty. The gold lettering on a blue background which may be seen on the cases today refers to a later arrangement because the Arts books would have been moved to Bodley's new Arts End upon its completion in 1612. The existing lettering indicates that at some time all the cases on the south side were devoted to Theology, together with the westernmost case on the north side. Then followed six cases of Law and two of Medicine. Some of the larger quarto books were shelved with the folios but the smaller ones, together with the octavos, were kept under lock and key in two 'closets' at the east end of the room which today are staff studies. There were seven shelves on each side. A number of books of special value or rarity were kept in the two cupboards with doors of open metalwork which are adjacent to the closets, labelled Arch E and Arch F, the contents of which the Librarian was compelled by statute to give out with his own hands. By 1604 the problem of space, particularly for the smaller volumes, was becoming acute and many were piled on the floors of the two studies. Bodley's first idea to provide extra storage was to place 'chests' in the windows and Thomas Key, the joiner who was normally employed in the Library, was instructed to make a specimen at his own expense, but the matter was not pursued. Instead, a gallery was constructed over the entrance door at the west end of the Library, probably by Thomas Key, and its breadth was 4ft. 5in. By August 1608 it was already overfull but not until the completion of Arts End was relief forthcoming.[17]

The weather in July 1601 was unusually hot and as there were no opening windows the ventilation in the Library must have been inadequate. Bodley was asked about the possibility of installing some casements but he took no immediate action saying that when the current heatwave was over there would be little cause for complaint for another twelve months. Further references to casements occur in letters to James. In August 1602 he was asked to arrange for John Smith, the 'chainman' to attend at the Library 'with his lockes and casements'; in June 1603 a decision had to be made about the positions in which two were to be installed before the Encaenia, but not in the east window which, Bodley thought, would be unfitting; and in May 1605 the insertion of further casements was under consideration.[18]

It was not only the structure of the Library and the books in it which received Bodley's attention. He was very much concerned with the day-to-day running and kept a close eye on his Librarian, giving him instructions on cataloguing, book selection and the position of books on the shelves, and also on domestic matters. James had to do almost everything himself, his only help at first being a man who cleaned and performed miscellaneous duties, for which he was paid 13s. 4d. each quarter.[19] An under-keeper was appointed in 1606, Philip Price, later Fellow of Brasenose, at a yearly salary of £6 13s. 4d. but he was not empowered to act as deputy librarian. On each occasion when the Librarian was absent a special deputy was appointed. Price resigned in 1613 and was succeeded by John Berry of Exeter College.[20] Before the Library had opened Bodley told James that it must have a bell and a clock. In the draft of the statutes which he drew up for the governance of the Library were stated the hours during which it would be open.

At these prescribed houres he [the Librarian] shall also cause to be rong the Warning-bell of his ingresse and egresse, that men may shunne the discommodities of repairing thither ouersoone, or abiding there too long, which the difference of clockes may occasion very often, to the preiudice and hindrance of himself as wel as others.[21]

A clock was not immediately provided but a bell was delivered in 1604. For some reason it proved to be unsatisfactory and Bodley had it recast in 1611. It probably hung in the bellcote at the south-west corner of the Library which is shown in David Loggan's engraving of 1675 (Ill. 21). It was taken down in 1747–8 and lay undetected under a staircase until 1866 when it was rehung in an iron frame in Selden End. Today it hangs again in the south-west corner of Duke Humfrey's Library though now beneath the roof and not above it, and it is still used to warn readers of the approach of closing time.[22]

David Loggan's engraving of the interior of the Library shows two globes, one on either side at the east end of the Library (Ill. 22). These were acquired by Bodley in 1601 at a cost of £20. He proposed that their dust-hoods ('globe-cases') should be raised by means of cords attached to them which would pass through pulley-wheels fastened to the roof, on the other ends of which would be counterpoise weights, this being the method in use at All Souls College. James was asked to estimate the length of cord which would be required. The globes, however, became something of a nuisance. When James I visited the Library in 1605 Bodley ordered that they should be put up in the gallery or in some other safe place. In 1608 he said that they were of little use, there was no proper place for them, and they should be sold for what they would fetch, the proceeds to be spent on books. However, a number of students protested against this and Bodley relented but not without further complaint about the lack of space to house them.[23] A coloured marble bust of Bodley himself was presented to the Library in 1605 by the Chancellor of the University, Thomas Sackville, Earl of Dorset.[24] There is no mention of it in Bodley's letters to James so that we do not know if he had any views on where it should be placed, but in Loggan's engraving it is shown mounted on the south wall of the Library. There is still a recess in that wall over the second window from the east (now partly concealed by the portrait of Dervorguilla Balliol) which was almost certainly its original position. The wall of the arch at the east end of the Library where it now rests is shown blank in Loggan and the bust was probably not placed there until about 1693 when it had to be removed from its original home to make way for the south gallery erected in that year. At the time the bust was presented the arch contained the great east window of the Library. The bust of King Charles I which sits in the niche on the right-hand side, opposite that of Bodley, was presented by Archbishop Laud in 1636 but removed during the Commonwealth. It was restored to its place in 1661 when £1 12s. 6d. was paid 'for polishing ye rust from ye King's Picture and setting it up againe in the Librarie'.[25]

In the early years of James's tenure of office as Librarian he consulted Bodley on minor domestic matters. He must have complained, early in 1603, about readers spitting in the Library. Bodley's answer was that there was no remedy except a more diligent approach to his duties by the cleaner.[26] Two months later an infestation of woodworm in the desks was reported and mould on the bindings of the books. Again the answer was short: nothing could be done about the worms and as to the mould, in return for the money he was paid, the cleaner 'should not onely sweepe the Libr. but, at the lest twice a quarter, with cleane clothes strike away the dust and mouldring of the bookes'.[27] One further example of Bodley's domesticity must suffice. Before the visit of King James I in 1605 he wrote to his Librarian 'I doe desire that after the Libr. is well swept,

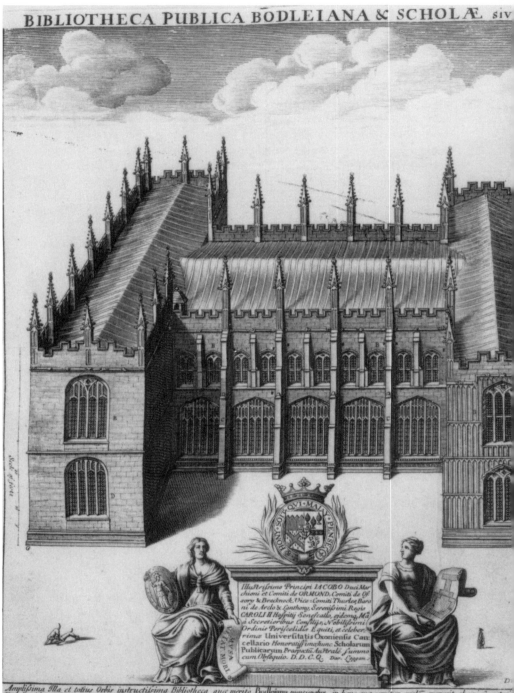

Illustrissimo Principi IACOBO Duci Marchioni et Comiti de ORMOND, Comiti de Ofsory & Brecknock, Vice-Comiti Thurlæ Baroni de Aedo & Lanthony, Serenissimi Regis
CAROLI II Hospitij Senescallo, ejidemq, Māi Secretioribus Consilijs, Nobilissimi
Ordinis Periscelidis Equiti, et celeberrima Universitatis Oxoniensis Cancellario Honoratissimum hunc Scholarum
Publicarum Prospectū Australi Summo
cum Obsequio. D.D.C.Q. Dav. Loggan.

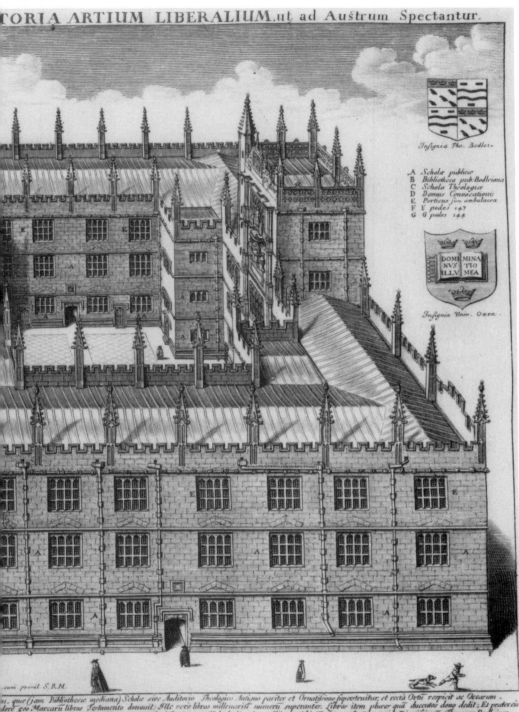

Insignia Tho. Bodleii.

A Scholæ publicæ
B Bibliotheca pub Bodleiana
C Schola Theologiæ
D Domus Consecrationis
E Porticus sive ambulacra
F E pedes 147
G G pedes 144

DOMI MINA
NVS TIO
ILLV MEA

Insignia Univ. Oxon.

cum privil. S.R.M.

...si, quæ (jam Bibliothecæ mechana) Scholæ sive Auditorio Theologico Autumno pariter et Ornatissimo superstruitur, et rectà Ortú respicit ac Occasum.
...dore 500 Marcarũ libros Testamento donauit. Ille vero libros millenariũ numerũ superantes. Libros item plures quã ducentos dono dedit: Et præter eũ
Nihil intus præter nudos parietes superedet. Instauratorẽ habuit virũ Honoratissimũ perpetuãq Memoria Dignissimũ Thomam Bodleium
Mauritio Comiti Dignitate proximum. Hic (inquã) collapsã Bibliothecã integritati restituit, et omnissenã Librorũ Sigelectile adornavit.
...liter an. 1612. dicti Bodley sumptibus ab humo erecta est, et Monumentis Libraryã locupletata Poeticas Orientalis ad. Aučtũ & Boreũ expor...
...axima Literarũ dispendio) fato egit. Et paulo poft, circa Añ. 1616 (variorũ Benefactorũ collatis Symbolis) ad Bibliothecã plagã Orientali...
...unificentissime Bodleius ulterius apud se designatũ Negotiũ ita penus comparârat, ut (legati inepti penuriæ summâ) propriæ poft morte...
...stet. Fundatorũ Colleg: Aliorũmq, Doctorũ virorum exhibere Effigies plurimas. Postremo circa Añ. 1636. sumptibus Universitatis
...bliothecæ Figura (præter Scholarũ Fabricam) non sit absimilis liteere H. Et hoc modo absoluta est incentissimã molis fabricæ, qualem...
...dice aspexeris. Inter Quas primas facile obtinent Gul: Laud Archiepiscopus Cantuariensis, Gul: Herbert Comes Pembrochianus, Kenelmus...
...dice sané infimo loco accensetur est vir Clarissimus Ioh: Seldenus ex interiori Templo apud Londinates Iuͬ Doctissimus, Cujus Privata (sed...

and the bookes cleansed from dust, yow would cause the floure to be well washed and dried and after rubbed with a litle rosemary: for a stronger sente I should not like.'[28]

Duke Humfrey's Library ceased to exist in isolation and lost its east window when Bodley built Arts End in 1610–12. Its completion, followed by his death in the following year, gave his Librarian both the opportunity and the space to carry out a major rearrangement of the books. James had always wanted the manuscripts to be kept separate from the printed books but Bodley had insisted upon shelving them together so that all the larger volumes, although safely chained, were immediately available to readers under what would be called today 'the open-access system'. Immediately after Bodley's death, however, James had his way. The manuscripts were removed from the 'open shelves', chains and all, and placed under lock and key in the gallery at the west end of the Library, the octavo books previously shelved there having been removed to the new Arts End. Readers now had to ask for the manuscripts to be fetched for them by the under-keeper. Some found this restriction to be exceedingly tiresome. The Keeper of the University Archives, Brian Twyne, was so incensed that he addressed a protest to the Curators of the Library whose agreement, he said, was required by the Librarian before making any changes in the disposition of the books. Twyne pointed out that the removal of the manuscripts had left unsightly gaps on the shelves in the floor-cases; that the printed catalogue (of 1605) was now useless; that the gallery had a stone wall (which suggests that the bookcases had no wooden backs) and was, therefore, 'a more dankish place' than downstairs; that the larger volumes could not now stand upright because the shelves had been designed for octavo books; that the under-keeper (then John Berry, newly-appointed in 1613) now had additional responsibility thrust upon him which he was insufficiently skilled to bear; and that 'the Manuscripts, by lugginge them vp and downe when they are called for, are more subiect to hurt and tearinge

21. The exterior of the Divinity School and Bodleian Library from the south showing the bell-turret. (From D. Loggan, *Oxonia Illustrata*, 1675)

22. The interior of Duke Humfrey's Library from Arts End and from Selden End. (From D. Loggan, *Oxonia Illustrata*, 1675)

and rumplinge then they were before, especially beinge encumbred with their chaynes seruinge to no purpose, but to makinge a noise and encumbrance.' James's reply when faced with this was that the Curators had, in fact, given him permission to move the manuscripts into the gallery because there was insufficient room for them below. However, after resisting for some time, he finally gave in and the manuscripts were restored to their original places.[29]

In his will Bodley directed that the greater part of his estate should be used for extending the Library in three specific ways.[30] The foundation stone of the new Schools Quadrangle was laid on 30 March 1613, the day after his funeral, and the first of his requests vitally affected the form of this building which was to be two-storeys high. He wished that a third storey should be added 'to goe in compasse round about the Scholes & so meete at each end in two Lobies or passages framed with some speciall comlines of workman- shippe to make a faire enterance into ye northe & Southe corners of my late new enlargement Estward' (i.e. Arts End).[31] Two further requests were set out in the will which were the 'raising of a faire storie case to make ye ascent more easye & gracefull to ye first great Librarie [i.e. Duke Humfrey], and thirdly about the performance of some bewtifull enlargment at the west end of the said Librarie towards Exeter Coll:' (now Selden End).[32] The position of the new staircase was not clearly defined but William Hackwell, one of Bodley's executors who, one assumes, would have been aware of his intentions, urged the University to build it in conjunction with the proposed extension at the west end of the Library. The plan for it became sufficiently firm to warrant the commissioning of a model from the mason, Hugh Davis, but nothing came of it. The old stone staircases in the turrets almost certainly continued to be the sole means of access to the Library as a whole until at least 1634 when they had to be demolished to make room for the Convocation House with Selden End over it. The new approaches from the Quadrangle stair- cases to Arts End were probably made to coincide with the removal of the stone staircases, and not before.[33]

The construction of Selden End (1634–40) completed the major structural changes to Duke Humfrey. It involved the demolition of most of the west wall with the gallery and its shelves for smaller books, and the outer porch with its turret staircases. Bodley's intentions had finally been carried out. Sixty years later it became

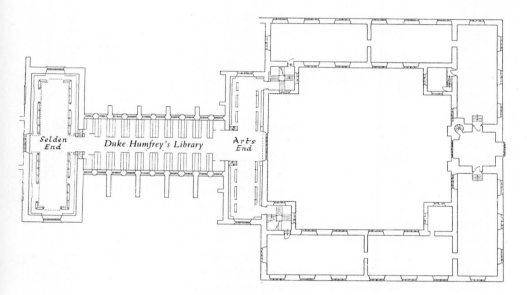

FIGURE 2. The Old Bodleian Library

evident that the south wall of Duke Humfrey, whose east and west walls had been deliberately removed in the past, was in imminent danger of collapse. In the interim the Library passed practically unscathed through the troublous years of the Civil War, and owed its preservation to Thomas, Lord Fairfax who, at his death in 1671, bequeathed to it a number of valuable manuscripts. John Aubrey, in his *Brief Lives*, wrote about him:

When Oxford was surrendered [24 June, 1646], the first thing General Fairfax did was to sett a good Guard of Soldiers to preserve the Bodleian Library. Tis said there was more hurt donne by the Cavaliers (during their Garrison) by way of Embezilling and cutting off chaines of bookes, then there was since. He was a lover of Learning, and had he not taken this speciall care, that noble Library had been utterly destroyed, for there were ignorant Senators enough who would have been contented to have had it so.[34]

Gifts to the Library had not been numerous from 1640 onwards but an increase began in 1657[35] and the problems of housing a growing number of books were never far distant. An extremely large bequest from Thomas Barlow, Bodley's Librarian from 1652 to 1660 and afterwards Bishop of Lincoln, which reached the Library in 1693,[36] made necessary the provision of additional shelving. This was achieved by the construction of a gallery over the floor-cases on the south side of Duke Humfrey (Ill. 23). At the same time a corresponding gallery was erected on the north side in which were placed the law books.[37] The galleries were completed in June 1693 and the Vice-Chancellor's Computus for 1692–3 shows that Roger Judge was paid £4. 15s. 0d. 'for 760 foot of bords used in the Library'.[38] Barlow's books, however, were not placed in the south gallery until 1696.[39] The galleries were not supported in any way from the floor of the Library nor did they rest upon the tops of the existing bookcases. The rear ends of the joists supporting their floors were let into the walls and their fronts were suspended from the roof timbers by metal straps. Access to these galleries was obtained by oak staircases constructed inside the staff studies at the east end of Duke Humfrey. The positions of the treads of the stairs were revealed on the walls behind the woodwork of the studies when it was temporarily removed during the restoration work of the 1960s. It was possible also to reach the galleries by way of the stairs then leading to those in

BIBLIOTHECÆ BODLEIANÆ   OXONIÆ Prospectus interior.

23. The interior of Duke Humfrey's Library from Arts End showing the north and south galleries. (After Loggan. Enlarged from a vignette in the 1738 *Catalogus impressorum Librorum Bibliothecæ Bodleianæ*)

Selden End but this route was apparently more hazardous.[40] About the time of their completion 'it was observed, that in the roof of the Library over the Divinitie School most of the great Beames were fled from the Wall'. Under the direction of the Vice-Chancellor, Henry Aldrich, Dean of Christ Church, himself a gifted architect, the beams were anchored on both sides.[41] By 1700, however, it had become evident that the building itself was in grave danger. For a hundred years heavy bookcases and an ever-increasing number of books had been housed in a room whose floor was not designed to take the weight imposed upon it and whose walls were already bearing the burden of the thrust of a heavy vault in the Divinity School below. The new galleries and their contents can only have aggravated the situation. The south wall of Duke Humfrey was found to be bulging outwards and the vault of the School was badly cracked. Accordingly, in February 1700 the Vice-Chancellor, Roger Mander, Master of Balliol, despatched David Gregory, the Savilian Professor of Astronomy, to London to consult Sir Christopher Wren, whose advice was quickly forthcoming. The foundations on the south side should be excavated and strengthened with ramping arches underground; a sewer should be constructed to carry away the rain-water from the roof so that it could not collect in stagnant pools and soak into the foundations; oaken wedges should be driven into the cracks in the Divinity School vault; broken mouldings should be made up with plaster of Paris and cracks filled with like material; and, finally, the work should be done in May and June so that all would be dry before the winter.[42] On 28 May 1700 a report was submitted by Thomas Robinson, the University mason, George Smith, the carpenter, and Thomas Young, the smith, upon their inspection of the building. They found that the buttresses were in a perfectly sound condition and they did not believe that there was any fault in them. They attributed the bulging of the wall to the tight bracing of the roof timbers carried out earlier by Aldrich, and proposed merely to anchor the floor beams which were resting upon the crowns of the arches of the vault below 'without any knocking, or otherwise shakeing the Arches, and will with care Observe their directions in wedging & pointing the said roof in all parts where there is occasion, and doe their utmost to preserve the beauty of the said roof'.[43] Gregory sent this report to Wren who, in his reply of 20 June 1700, expressed the opinion that, since the fault to be corrected was the bulging of the wall, he did not see that the anchoring of the floor-beams would be of much use, and he asked for a more particular account of the movement of the wall and of the roof timbers.[44] This was duly prepared and sent to him by Gregory on 16 July. It is worth quoting in full:

THE WORKMENS REPORT CONCERNING THE DIVINITY SCHOOL & LIBRARY.
OXON. 13 JULY 1700

The Buttresses on the North side toward the Theater are every way greater & stronger than those on the south side to which the building draws
The clear of the building at the bottom is 30½ feet, on the Library floor 30 feet ten inches and where the roof is sett on 31 feet 1 inch
The North wall is perpendicular, so that all the giving is on the south side. The south wall leans outward or overhangs from top to bottom 7½ inches so

that the beams are drawn out of both walls: to prevent which going further about seven years ago, three of the four beams of the roof were anchored

The posts which rest on the Corbells are about 2½ inches from the wall. But the flying off of the wall is more apparent from the walls leaving the stalls of the Library which is about 3½ inches at the top of the stalls & 2¼ at bottom. That the Stalls were once close to the walls (at least not much distant from them) is apparant from their being nail'd to the wall: which Nails are now drawn

All these givings are greater toward the midle and less toward the ends of the building: the ends being kept in by the buildings at each end

About seven or eight years since, there were Gallerys hang'd on each side of this part of the Library that is over the Divinity School. One end of the joysses of the Gallery is lett into the wall and the other hang'd by irons to the brasses of the roof

Each of the four great Arches of the Vault is cracked on the south rib, a litle above the place where the Cramps and bolts that were putt in by Sr Christopher Wren's Direction for sustaining the springers of the arches, doe reach

The Crack is continued all the length of the Divinity School, and since the last time that it was fill'd up with cement, about 7 or 8 years since, it is opened near an inch

Several stones of the vault, all along by the crack, are in hazard to drop: But the workmen deferr the wedging or pinning up the crack, untill by anchoring, or some other means proposed by Sr Christopher Wren, the further giving of the building is prevented

What the Workmen propose is to anchor the beams that ly upon the crowns of the Arches, so that the anchors may take in the whole buttresses; by which means they pretend to keep the walls from flying farther assunder[45]

On 23 July Wren acknowledged the receipt of this report. He remained convinced that the only way to correct the bulging south wall was by strengthening the buttresses in some way, but first of all the floor joists should be inspected because he feared that they might be exerting undue pressure on the stonework of the vault below. 'I am loath,' he said, 'to advise the moving of the Bookes & Classes, but I thinke it can hardly be avoyded, but certainly the Floor must be searched, and noe Girders should touch the Vault.' He suggested two methods of stabilizing the building. The first was to brace the opposite buttresses together 'by two Rods of Iron keyed together upon the outsides or Backs of the Buttresses; these must be good Swedish Iron inch & halfe square, three lengthes will reach over . . .; by such methods I braced the lofty Spire of Salisbury, after the Lightening had rent it with Cracks of 200 foot long.' The iron rods should be forged in Portsmouth where the most skilled anchor-smiths were to be found. The second method, which he believed would be the cheaper, was that which was adopted—the construction of additional buttresses to support the existing ones but on no account to be bonded to them.[46] He provided drawings of both methods (Ill. 24) in the second of which may be seen the position of the galleries and the metal struts by which the standing bookcases were to be trussed to the wall, to which reference will be made below.[47] Having considered Wren's suggested additional buttresses and the drawing thereof the University mason, Robinson, had the temerity to propose an alternative construction and to provide a drawing of it.[48] His suggestion was that the ramping arches, shown in Wren's drawing as being underground, should rise much higher to the point on the existing buttresses from which the arches of the vault sprang.

The Vice-Chancellor called in two outside advisers to mediate: Mr Townsend, the mason, and Mr Mein, the carpenter. They advised against Robinson's alternative plan and were in favour of the insertion of an entirely new floor which would stand clear of the vault, together with the iron tie-rods, but these were to be half an inch thick and three inches wide. They considered that these could be made just as easily in Oxford as in Portsmouth. Moreover, Mein disapproved of Wren's suggested method of joining the rods together and proposed instead a left-hand and right-hand screw, of which he provided a drawing.[49] The University carpenter, Smith, was asked if he could make a floor capable of bearing the necessary weight which would not have to rest upon the vault. His response was that it could not be done with oak beams but it would be possible with fir. Neither he nor Robinson, however, was in favour of this because the walls and buttresses would be greatly weakened by the large number of deep holes which would have to be made in them to take the fir beams. They proposed that the floor should continue to rest upon the vault and that the plan for the higher ramping arches to support the south wall should be carried out. Townsend and Mein disagreed. They insisted that however firmly the walls were buttressed from

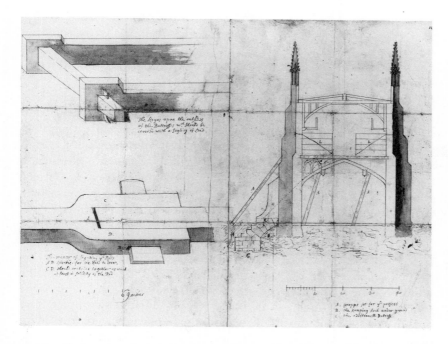

24. Sir Christopher Wren's proposals for strengthening the building either with additional buttresses on the south side or with tie-rods. (MS Bodl. 907, fols. 13, 14)

without the weight of the books and bookcases would crush the vault.[50]

Wren's observations upon these various proposals were brief and perhaps a little condescending in tone. He concluded them by saying 'I might be more particular in these directions, but I suppose I have to doe with ingenious Artists, to whom it will be enough to explain my reasons in generall.' He was not prepared to make any concessions. He had thought, he said, of an 'archbutten', a flying buttress, but had rejected the idea on the grounds that it would have been more expensive and that it would have been perishable because rain-water penetrated the joints—'the ruine of all the Cathedralls in England begins upon this account (I have 70 of them at Westminster to rebuild).' He proposed to repair the cracked vault of the Divinity School and to replace any damaged stone 'but how to doe this underneath without opening the floor above is what will require Art, wch is not usually practised, but may securely be done'. He went on to say 'I dare not advise a new Floor to the Library, because there is not highth enough between the Floor & the top of the vault to trusse up the Girders' but he proposed to lessen the weight borne by the existing floor by trussing the bookcases up to the walls with iron stays (marked L in his drawing), thus reducing the danger of the vault being crushed and perhaps even drawing the wall in rather than thrusting it out. He agreed that the insertion of a new floor would severely damage the walls but was critical of Mein's alternative method of joining iron tie-rods: 'The twohanded Screw is a pretty Knack and usefull in some cases. . . . The threads of the Screw will be stript off, or the Nutt ript open with much lesse weight, as I have experimented.'[51]

Work eventually began in May 1701. Priority was given to the additional buttresses, starting with the westernmost. The foundation of the first was 21 ft. deep, that is, 10 ft. below the foundation of the building. The foundations of the next two were 19 ft. deep and of the fourth, the easternmost, 16 ft. (Ill. 25). This work was completed by September 1701 and during the winter the bookcases were trussed up to the walls. This involved the boring of holes right through the stonework to take the metal struts, the exterior ends of which were secured to irons let into the wall. Work on the Divinity School vault began in the summer of 1702. Its condition and treatment were described thus:

It was very faulty, and in many places like to tumble and drop. The wide Seames of the main Arches were filled with Lead, the small Seames with Oyster Shells. In some places the stones were taken out, and whole larger stones put in their place. The larger Seames were wedged up with well seasoned oaken wedges of 6, 9, or 12 inches long. The small broken Mouldings were made good with Plaister of Paris, the larger with Stone. The little statues in the Pendants (which were loose before, and was the cause why many had droped in brushing the roof, and had been broken) were fixed with mortar.

The vault was then whitened with stone dust.[52]

Duke Humfrey's Library saw few changes during the eighteenth century. Soon after his appointment as Bodley's Librarian in 1719 Joseph Bowles installed shelving below the desks and began a complicated rearrangement of the books which, basically, involved removing the quarto books from the folio shelves and placing them in a separate sequence in the new lower shelves. The resultant gaps in

25. Sir Christopher Wren's additional buttresses on the south wall of the
building. (Thomas-Photos, Oxford)

the folio shelves were filled with volumes from elsewhere and,
although Bowles kept a record of what he was doing, considerable
chaos reigned for a time.[53] The Library was very little used between
1730 and 1740. Rarely were more than two books issued to readers in
a day and for days on end none at all.[54] In 1756 the comfort of readers

was increased by the purchase of six walnut chairs at 16*s*. each and 36 Windsor chairs at 8*s*. 6*d*. each. The old fixed benches between the bookcases were banished and, as a natural consequence, between 1757 and 1761 the chains were removed from the folio books.[55] Heating was introduced into the Library for the first time in 1821. Hot air was conveyed through two small gratings at the west end from a stove outside. This was totally ineffectual and only those in close proximity to the gratings received any benefit whatsoever. A boiler and steam pipes were installed in 1845 by James Park at an estimated cost of about £150 plus carriage, fixing, and expenses but they proved to be unsatisfactory and were replaced by hot-water pipes in 1863.[56] The system continued to be inadequate because the fire was extinguished every evening and relit every morning.[57]

The appearance of Duke Humfrey in 1845 was not very different from that of today, except that the galleries of 1693 were still in position along the north and south walls. The floor of the central gangway was lower than that of Arts End so that one stepped down into it, and the bookcases on either side were on a higher level.[58] The frames on the ends of the bookcases intended for the display of lists of the books on the shelves were filled with Oxford Almanacks. The first two and last two alcoves on either side were screened off each by a pair of lattice doors backed by green curtains. They were reserved for the use of privileged readers. Some of the doors are still in use.[59] The pillared doors to the two staff studies at the west end are probably of a later date. They were preceded by plain cupboard doors.[60] In 1875 fears were once again expressed about the stability of the building and Douglas Galton, an engineer and Director of Public Works and Buildings, was called in to advise. His report was alarming: the roof needed repair, the floor was too weak to bear its load and was resting on the vault of the Divinity School below, and the south wall had bulged about five inches in the centre of its length. The situation was very similar to that which Wren had found in 1700 and which his additional buttresses were intended to rectify. Work began in July 1876 and the Library was cleared of furniture. When the floor was removed its framework was found to be resting entirely on the vault but the latter required only minimal repair. Wren's oyster shells and wooden wedges were removed and replaced with stone. All crevices were cleared and grouted with Portland cement and the stones were reset in one portion of the central main transverse rib which had sunk considerably. Galton reported that the vault was 'now in a perfectly sound and satisfactory state'.

Galton's remedy for the bulging south wall was the other of the two which Wren had considered but had not chosen—the insertion of wrought-iron tie-rods to link the north and south walls. Four were inserted at both floor and roof level, 1½ in. square, the size which Wren would have used. Some of the old floor joists were used again, but five new English oak girders 14 in. by 12 in., each trussed with two wrought-iron rods 2 in. in diameter, were introduced, four of them over the four main transverse arches of the vault. The whole floor was thus raised above the vault of the Divinity School so that no part rested upon it. For reasons of economy and because they would be covered with matting the new floor-boards were of deal and not of oak as in the past. The new floor level was 5 in. above that of Arts End instead of below it as formerly. The decayed portions of the roof were renewed and the side galleries were removed, never to return.[61] Their removal restored the shell of the room to its original early-seventeenth-century appearance but Bodley's large bookcases themselves came under threat. Having seen Duke Humfrey without them during the period of repairs to the floor a majority of the Curators of the Library in October 1876 decided not to replace them. Six were already in a parlous state. Their ends had been sawn off, they had been knocked to pieces, and the fragments piled up in Selden End or stacked away with other old wood in the basement of the Sheldonian Theatre. The Librarian, H. O. Coxe, was totally opposed to the Curators' plan and T. G. Jackson was called in to advise. In the light of his unfavourable reaction to it the Curators reluctantly agreed to reinstate the cases on a temporary basis for a period, suggested by Benjamin Jowett, of one year. However, the matter was not allowed to drop. A committee was set up, presided over by Jowett, to report, in general, upon the arrangements of Library rooms. 'In dealing with Duke Humfrey it recommended that books should be kept separate from readers, and that readers should be allowed ample space, provided with shelves and drawers, and parted off by a low case from their neighbours an arrangement which would have involved a clean sweep of the old fittings.' The Curators would not go quite as far as this but agreed that the height of the new fittings should not exceed five feet. Fortunately the University's Hebdomadal Council threw out the proposal by fifteen votes to four.[62]

The removal of the galleries in Duke Humfrey left expanses of blank wall on either side. These were now adorned with a series of portraits of the founders of colleges, which formerly hung in the Picture Gallery (now the Bodleian Upper Reading Room). They possess no particular artistic merit and some are supposed to be imaginary. The likeness of John Balliol is said to have been based on that of a local blacksmith,[63] and his wife Dervorguilla on that of Jenny Reeves, the daughter of Henry Reeves, an Oxford apothecary of the parish of St Peter in the East.[64] They are believed to have been painted about 1670 and, until the present century, were attributed to a Dutch artist, William Sunman or Sonmans. It is now known that they were commissioned by the colleges as gifts to the Bodleian Picture Gallery and that the painter of some, if not all, was John Taylor, a local man who was Mayor of Oxford in 1695. Twenty-one portraits now hang on the walls of Duke Humfrey, 10 on the south side and 11 on the north, all but 3 of which formed part of the original series.[65] For the next eighty years or so no major work was carried out on the structure of the building but some renewals and interior changes took place in Duke Humfrey. In 1913 a donation of £10 was spent on modifying some of the old seats 'without impairing their appearance or use' so that twelve additional readers could be accommodated.[66] After the war, in 1920–1, some of the pinnacles were found to be unsafe and one or two actually dangerous. These, together with dilapidated buttresses in the north side, were repaired;[67] a further pinnacle on the north side had to be rebuilt in Clipsham stone in 1958.[68] In addition, in 1921 a thick growth of ivy, which covered the south wall of the Divinity School and Library, was removed.[69] In 1926 the roof was found to be seriously affected by woodworm and dry rot and repairs were carried out by the University. Confirmation was given to the belief that the main portion of the roof dated from the fifteenth century.[70] Electric lighting was introduced into the Old Library reading rooms for the first time in 1929.[71] In Duke Humfrey overall lighting was provided by ornamental globes supported by wooden standards which were placed at intervals on the tops of the bookcases (Ill. 26). They were presumably designed to give a Jacobean effect which was, in fact, not

26. Duke Humfrey's Library before 1960 showing the lighting introduced in 1929. (Thomas-Photos, Oxford)

unpleasing, but the concealed strip-lighting which superseded them thirty years later is less obtrusive and much more effective, revealing, as it does, the full glory of the painted ceiling. Lighting for the desks was provided, as it is today, by individual lamps.

During the Second World War Duke Humfrey once again became a great empty room because all its earlier books were removed in 1941 to the comparative safety of the New Library where they remained until June 1945.[72] During the Long Vacation of 1953 a further modernization took place. The old 'greenhouse' heating pipes of 1863, which had continued to emit a vague warmth into Duke Humfrey for ninety years, were removed and a new installation took their place, more effective and less unsightly than its predecessor.[73] In 1956 the floor timbers of the Old Library, including Duke Humfrey, were examined and found to have suffered at some time from damp and attack by woodworm. Although neither seemed to be active it was decided to remove all the woodwork showing such signs and to give all the timbers a complete preservative treatment. At the same time the electrical wiring was renewed and additional lights were installed.[74]

In 1958 the floor of the Library was, for the third time, found to be in a serious condition and once again resting on the vault of the Divinity School, a situation not apparently detected during the inspection of 1956 (Ill. 27). Major restoration was necessary, as a preliminary to which all the books and the bookcases had to be removed. This time the cases were more sympathetically treated than they had been in 1876. They were mounted on bogies and moved bodily to the north window of Selden End. They were then swung out by a travelling crane and lowered to the ground from where they were taken into the Proscholium for storage until the end of 1961. Wren's additional buttresses on the south side were removed (Ill. 28) and reinforced uprights were inserted in the original buttresses on both sides of the building. These, together with ring-beams and steel and concrete floors ensure that the structure is now rigid, further movement is impossible, and the vault of the Divinity School is safe at last from pressure from above. Bodley's bookcases were hoisted back by the same route as that by which they had been evacuated.[75] The small cases, previously containing reference books, which had been attached to their ends sometime in the nineteenth century were removed, and copies of the original frames used for display of the lists

27. In 1958 the floor beams of Duke Humfrey's Library, inserted in 1876, were found to be resting on the vault of the Divinity School. (Thomas-Photos, Oxford)

of the contents of the seventeenth-century cases took their place. The walls having been cleaned, the windows reglazed using roundels from the west window of Selden End, and the painted ceiling restored (the whole cost of which was borne by the late Donald F. Hyde of New York) Duke Humfrey's Library is now as handsome in appearance as it has ever been since Thomas Bodley opened it in 1602, and the building of which it forms part has an overall strength which it has never before possessed. The completion of the restoration programme was celebrated on 18 May 1963 when an evening party was held in the Library and a programme of appropriate music was presented by members of the Library staff.

It is without exaggeration that one can echo the words which Sir Roger Wilbraham wrote in his Journal in September 1603 'The chiefest wonder in Oxford is a faire Divinitie School with Church windoes: and over it the fairest librarie called the Universitie Librarie

28. The south side of the building after the removal of Sir Christopher Wren's buttresses. (Thomas-Photos, Oxford)

founded & supplied daily by Mr. Bodley, that is thought for bewtie of building & wainscott frames & chaynes to kepe the books, will equall any in christendome.'[76]

NOTES

SOURCES

1. *Reg. Cong.* 415–7.

2. For a list of these letters see M. R. James, *A Descriptive Catalogue of the Manuscripts in the Library of Corpus Christi College, Cambridge,* ii (1911), 322–8.

INTRODUCTION

1. For the University's chests see *Reg. Cong.* 418–24.

2. For a full description of the building see Sir T. G. Jackson, *The Church of St Mary the Virgin Oxford* (1897), 90–106.

3. Among the archives of Oriel College is a document written in about 1367 describing the dispute. It has been published in C. R. L. Fletcher (ed.), *Collectanea,* (1885), 62–5 (OHS 5) and also in C. L. Shadwell and H. E. Salter (eds), *Oriel College Records* (1926), 24–7 (OHS 85).

4. *Reg. Cong.* 422.

5. A code of statutes governing the Library was drawn up in 1367. See *Mun. Acad.* i 226–8 and *Statuta,* 165–6.

6. *Mun. Acad.* i. 261–8; *Statuta,* 216–21.

NOTES TO CHAPTER ONE

1. *Ep. Acad.* i. 5.

2. Ibid. 10.

3. Ibid. 14.

4. *Dictionary of National Biography.*

5. A cell of thirteen Benedictines from the Monastery of St Peter in Gloucester was formed in Oxford in 1283. This developed into Gloucester Hall which, in turn, in 1714, became Worcester College.

6. *Ep. Acad.* i. 20.

7. One mark sterling was equivalent to 13*s*. 4*d*.

8. *Ep. Acad.* i. 52.

9. Ibid.

10. Ibid. 62.

11. Ibid. 242.

12. Ibid. 28, 31.

13. Ibid. 25, 26.

14. Ibid. 26.

15. Ibid. 22.

16. Ibid. 24. Wood (*Hist.* ii. 775) states that William Gray (d. 1436) was Dean but he was Bishop of London at the time.

17. Ibid. 28.

18. Ibid. 41.

19. Ibid. 55.

20. Ibid. 59. A similar order was made in 1448 by the commissioners elected to speed up the building work and to raise money for it (see p. 12). The granting of graces was a regular source of income. Money was paid by individuals to the University in return for permission to vary the requirements of the statutes and for other concessions. The system was open to abuse. There are numerous references to the granting of graces in the Register of Congregation, 1448–63 (Registrum Aa in the University Archives) in many of which the Divinity School is specifically mentioned. See *Reg. Cong. passim*.

21. *Ep. Acad.* 23.

22. H. E. Salter (ed.), *The Oxford Deeds of Balliol College* (1913), 150–5 (OHS 64); id., *Survey of Oxford*, i (1960), 56 (OHS NS 14).

23. School Street extended from High Street immediately west of St Mary's Church, through what is now St Mary's Entry, northwards to the city wall which ran parallel to what is now Broad Street.

24. Salter, *Balliol Deeds*, 29–30; id., *Survey*, ii (1969), 189, 90 (OHS NS 20).

25. Ibid. i. 57–8.

26. Emden, i. 379, 80; RCHM, 5.

27. This suggestion has been quoted verbatim from Myres p. 152. Much new light has been thrown upon its construction by Dr Myres's interpretation of the clues which came to light in the course of the work and the present writer is deeply indebted to him for much of the information on the building period which appears in this work.

28. E. A. Gee, 'Oxford masons, 1370–1530', *Archaeological Journal*, cix (1952), 69.

29. *Ep. Acad.* i. 46. Repeated on p. 58, but omitting the hay. English version in Hope, pp. 218–9.

30. *Statuta*, 257–8; *Reg. Cong.* 422.

31. Gee, op. cit. 74; *Mun. Acad.* ii. 595–7; *Reg. Canc.* i. 191–2.

32. *Ep. Acad.* i. 191–2. English version in Hope, pp. 219–20.

33. Cox, p. 49 n. 9. Myres (p. 153) suggests that the idea of a vault, or at least a vault of the height previously contemplated, could have been abandoned in 1444 when the decision to build an upper room was taken.

34. *Ep. Acad.* i. 244.

35. Myres, pp. 166–8.

36. *Ep. Acad.* i. 285.

37. *Reg. Cong.* 393.

38. *Ep. Acad.* i. 266; *Reg. Cong.* 397.

39. *Mun. Acad.* ii. 567–75 (with English summary); *Reg. Canc.* ii. 250–5; *Statuta*, 268–74. Regarding the granting of graces see also n. 20 above.

40. *Mun. Acad.* ii. 571.

41. Emden, i. 653. He was a Keeper of the Chest of Five Keys in 1449. At some point he had on loan from Henry Webber, Dean of Exeter Cathedral, a volume now in Bodley (MS Bodley 320, *SC* 2234).

42. Emden, i. 506. He also was a Keeper of the Chest of Five Keys in 1449.

43. Cox, p. 54; Emden, i. 421.

44. *Mun. Acad.* ii. 736–7.

45. *Ep. Acad.* i. 276. In Emden as 'Lyseux'.

46. Ibid. 275, 277.

47. Cox, pp. 54, 56.

48. *Ep. Acad.* i. 324.

49. Ibid. 321. Rede was a landowner of Borstall, Bucks. There are many references to him in White Kennetts's *Parochial antiquities* (1695) including, under the year 1447: 'The said Edmund Rede Esquire was now a special benefactor to the building of the Divinity School in Oxford, by contributing Timber and Stones from his adjacent woods and quarries' (p. 656).

50. *Ep. Acad.* i. 322. William, Lord Lovell (1397–1455) was also Lord Holand, a title he took on the death of his grandmother Maud Holand in 1423.

51. Ibid. 323.

52. Ibid. 326.

53. Among the muniments of University College. Published in Cox.

54. Cox, pp. 55, 58; Gee, op. cit. 72–3. Payments to Jannyns and to Atkyns are to be found in the accounts for the building of Merton College chapel, May 1448–May 1450. See J. E. T. Rogers (ed.), *Oxford City documents, 1268–1665* (1891), 314–37 (OHS 18).

55. Ibid.; Gee, op. cit., 112.

56. The noble was a gold coin equivalent to 6s. 8d. or 10s.

57. *Reg. Cong.* 294.

58. *Mun. Acad.* ii. 739. The Chest of Five Keys was the main repository of the University's cash and current records. It is now in the Ashmolean Museum.

59. Publ. in *Med. Arch.* ii. 272–358.

60. Ibid. 295.

61. Ibid.

62. Myres, p. 154.

63. *Med. Arch.* ii. 295 n. 1.

64. *Ep. Acad.* ii. 377. Beckington was a scholar and had been Duke Humfrey's chancellor from about 1420. In 1453 the University appealed to him for help in their attempt to obtain the books promised by the duke but never received (*Ep. Acad.* i. 318–19).

65. *Mun. Acad.* ii. 716–17; *Reg. Canc.* ii. 185; English version in Hope, p. 244.

66. *Med. Arch.* ii. 299.

67. *Ep. Acad.* ii. 383.

68. Ibid. 384.

69. Ibid. 390.

70. *Med. Arch.* ii. 303.

71. Ibid. 304.

72. Ibid. 307.

73. Ibid. 308.

74. Ibid. 315.

75. *Ep. Acad.* ii. 429–30.

76. *Med. Arch.* ii. 322.

77. *Ep. Acad.* ii. 432.

78. Ibid. 433–4.

79. Ibid. 437.

80. Ibid. 439–41.

81. Ibid. 438, 451, 453, 464, 472, 474, 477.

82. *Med. Arch.* ii. 291. The Chancellor in 1478 was Thomas Chaundeler and the Commissary Thomas Stevyn of Exeter College. For Orchard see Gee, op. cit. 75–9.

83. *Ep. Acad.* ii. 443.

84. Ibid. 446.

85. *Med. Arch.* ii. 323.

86. Ibid. 338.

87. Op. cit.

88. William Worcestre, *Itineraries*, ed. from MS CCC Cambridge 210 by J. H. Harvey (1969), 277.

89. *Pietas*, 10.

90. MS Bodl. 13, fol. 16^v (*SC* 3056).

91. Poole, ii. 48–9. This information stems from Anthony Wood. If it is correct this is the only known depiction of the staircase. The bust was made about 1615 when the staircase was still in use.

92. *Annual report, 1967–8*, 4.

93. Bodley to James, 223.

94. *Pietas*, p. 10 n.

95. *Ep. Acad.* ii. 470.

96. Ibid. 532–3.

97. Ibid. 544–5.

98. Ibid. 556.

99. Ibid. 556–7.

NOTES TO CHAPTER TWO

1. Bodl. MS Wood D 14, pp. 91–2 (*SC* 8548). See W. H. Turner (ed.), *The visitation of the County of Oxford* (1871), 84–7 (Harleian Soc. 5). The sketches are not reproduced but the editor has provided heraldic descriptions and has named many of them.

2. Bodl. MS Dugdale 11, fols. 146–7 (*SC* 6501). Fair copies of 29 of these sketches are to be found in Alderman William Fletcher's extra-illustrated copy of Wood, *Hist.* ii at pp. 781–3 (Bodl. MS Top. Oxon. c. 16).

3. Bodl. MS Wood F 33, fols. 111–12 (*SC* 8495).

4. Bodl. MS Top. Oxon. e. 286, fol. 27. According to a note in this MS by John Price (Bodley's Librarian 1768–1813), Greenwood transcribed it from Matthew Hutton's collection of arms which is now Bodl. MS Rawl. B 397 but this is not entirely correct because Greenwood included some Oxfordshire and Buckinghamshire churches not found in Hutton. Moreover, Hutton omitted the Divinity School but there is a blank leaf at the point where, in comparison with Greenwood, it should appear. It is entered in Hutton's index but without a page number. A list in an unidentified hand made about 1768, copied from Greenwood, names many of the shields (Bodl. MS Top. Oxon. e. 263, fols. 57–8).

5. Bodl. MS Wood F 2, pp. 50, 52 (*SC* 8464★).

6. Wood, *Hist.* ii. 781–3.

7. Engraved by Joseph Skelton and reproduced as the Oxford Almanack for 1816.

8. Hope, p. 233.

9. Bodl. MS Wood D 14, pp. 93–5 (*SC* 8548).

10. Bodl. MS Wood F 33, fols. 113–4 (*SC* 8495).

11. Bodl. MS Wood F 2, p. 52 (*SC* 8464*); Wood, *Hist.* ii. 783–6.

12. D. T. Powell, some notes and sketches, 1801 (Bodl. MS Top. Oxon. b. 256, fols. 45–60); Thomas Willement, a list of 86 shields, some identified, and 6 sketches, 1819–27 (Bodl. MS Top. gen. e. 78, pp. 320–4); Herbert Hurst, 1887 (Bodl. MS Top. Oxon. c. 183, fols. 886–93).

13. See Abbreviations s.v. Hope.

14. See Abbreviations s.v. Legge.

15. See Abbreviations s.v. RCHM.

16. Greening Lamborn's proof-sheets of the volume and his own copy are in the Bodleian (G.A. Oxon. 4° 691, 2) as is also his annotated copy of Legge (G.A. Oxon. 8° 1264).

17. *Notes and Queries*, cxci (1946), 71–3, 282.

18. *BQR* i (1914), 37.

19. Bodl. G.A. Oxon. b. 81. Other copies of some of the photographs are in Bodl. MS Top. Oxon. b. 268.

20. Hope, pp. 240–1.

21. Wood, *Hist.* i. 638. The University made strenuous efforts to bring about the admission to Oxford of Edmund de la Pole, son of the king's sister who was the wife of John de la Pole the University's High Steward. See *Ep. Acad.* ii. 453–7, 461, 463. When this had been achieved two letters (to which Wood refers) were sent by the University to the king (*Ep. Acad.* ii. 478, 483–4) heaping encomiums upon the boy 'of so fulsome, if not profane a character, that they cannot be received as testimony in his favour'. Thus they are described by H. A. Napier who has provided full English translations in his *Historical Notices of the Parishes of Swyncombe and Ewelme* (1858), 162–4.

22. Wood, *Hist.* ii. 786.

23. Hope, p. 238.

24. MS Bodl. 42 (*SC* 1846).

NOTES TO CHAPTER THREE

1. Details about the requirements for these degrees are to be found in A. Clark (ed.), *Register of the University of Oxford*, ii, pt. 1 (1887) particularly pp. 109, 10, 130–145, 194–217 (OHS 10).

2. There are in the Bodleian two photographs of the School, one of about 1872 and the other a little later, showing tables and chairs in position for an examination (G.A. Oxon. c. 98, fol. 18; G.A. Oxon. a. 44, p. 95).

3. MS CCC Cambridge 423, fol. 1. Printed in Wood, *Hist*. ii. 778 and in Hope, p. 229 with an English version.

4. Wood, *Hist*. ii. 780.

5. Ibid.

6. Ibid. 779–80.

7. R. W. Dixon, *History of the Church of England*, iv (1891), 187.

8. Ibid. 431. The Commissioners were Bishops John White of Lincoln, James Brooks of Gloucester, and John Holyman of Bristol.

9. A. Clark, *A Bodleian Guide for Visitors* (1906), 26–7.

10. Wood, *Life*, iv. 70.

11. For William Byrd see articles by Mrs J. C. Cole in *Oxoniensia*, xiv (1949), 63–74 and xvii/xviii (1954), 193–9.

12. RCHM 10.

13. M. G. Hobson (ed.), *Oxford Council Acts, 1666–1701* (1909), 213, 291. Wood, *Life*, *passim*.

14. Wood, *Life*, iv. 78.

15. RCHM 8.

16. Wood, *Life*, i. 479.

17. Ibid. iii. 161.

18. T. Hearne, *Remarks and Collections*, ed. D. W. Rannie, v (1901), 1 (OHS 42).

19. Wood, *Life*, ii. 828.

20. W. Roughead (ed.), *Trial of Mary Blandy* (1914), 35.

21. Craster, p. 124.

22. Ibid. 146, 346.

23. Ibid. 242.

24. Library Records c. 557.

25. *Annual Report, 1967–8,* 4.

NOTES TO CHAPTER FOUR

1. *Pietas,* 28–29.

2. Macray, p. 12.

3. C. W. Boase (ed.), *Register of the University of Oxford,* i (1884), 129 (OHS 1); A. B. Emden, *A Biographical register of the University of Oxford, 1501–1540* (1974).

4. Bodley to Univ. 4.

5. C. E. Mallet, *A History of the University of Oxford,* ii (1924), 83, 90, 91.

6. Wood, *Hist.* ii. 919.

7. Macray, p. 13; Mallet, op. cit. iii (1986), 465–6.

8. H. H. E. Craster, 'Schola Vetus Medicinae', *BQR* iii (1921), 148.

9. *Trecentale,* 19. Information about Sir Thomas Bodley is to be found in many places but see especially Philip, ch. 1.

10. Bodley to Univ. 4.

11. Ibid. 6.

12. *Calendar of State Papers domestic, 1598–1601* (1869), 174.

13. Myres, p. 165 n. 2.

14. RCHM 8, 9.

15. Bodley to James, 1.

16. Bodley to Univ. 7.

17. The description of the appearance of the Library at the beginning of the 17th cent. has been taken principally from Bodley's letters to James (particularly G. W. Wheeler's introduction), from *Pietas,* 9–11, and from *BQR* i (1914–16), 280–2.

18. Bodley to James, 9, 52, 92, 139.

19. Bodley to James, 18 n. 2.

20. Bodley to James, 111 n. 5.

21. Bodley to James, 55; *Trecentale*, 40.

22. For a description and photograph of the bell see F. Sharpe, 'Bodley's bell', *BLR* iii (1950–2), 143–6. See also Macray, pp. 42–3.

23. Bodley to James, 7, 8, 147, 151, 181–3, 221.

24. Poole, i. 28.

25. Ibid. 44–5.

26. Bodley to James, 76.

27. Ibid. 84.

28. Ibid. 150–1.

29. G. W. Wheeler, '"Free access" in 1613', *BQR* iv (1923–5), 192–8.

30. The will is printed in full in Macray, pp. 402–18. Extracts relating to the Library are in *Trecentale*, 65–86.

31. Macray, p. 406.

32. Ibid. 407.

33. See I. G. Philip, 'The building of the Schools Quadrangle', *Oxoniensia*, xiii (1948), 39–48. It must not be assumed that the western staircases in the Quadrangle originally ascended to Bodley's third storey. It is likely that they gave access only to the first floor of the Schools, as did those in the eastern corners, until 1634 when the stone staircases at the west end of Duke Humfrey were demolished. Access to Bodley's new gallery would have been through two newly-made openings (about 1617) in the corners of Arts End into his 'lobies' from which two short staircases would have led up to it. The Library would have been entirely self-contained. There is visible evidence today that alterations were at some time made to the main staircases. (See J. N. L. Myres, 'Oxford libraries in the seventeenth and eighteenth centuries', in F. Wormald and C. E. Wright (eds.), *The English Library before 1700* (1958), p. 254, n. 30.)

34. Bodl. MS Aubrey 8, fol. 60.

35. Macray, p. 125.

36. Philip, p. 65.

37. Macray, p. 158.

38. Wood, *Life*, iii. 426, iv. 84.

39. Curators' Minutes, 24 Feb. 1695/6 (Library Records e. 3).

40. Macray, p. 269; 'Recollections of the Library in 1863', by H. J. Shuffrey (Library Records d. 1794); Library Records c. 1786, Photo 156. RCHM (p. 8) records that 'High up in the E. wall [of Duke Humfrey] are two square-headed doorways, probably inserted in 1692–3 to give access to the galleries, and now blocked.' The outlines of the openings are still visible as one looks eastwards from Duke Humfrey but the assumption that they were inserted in 1692–3 is not borne out by an early-18th-cent. engraving (Ill. 23) which shows the galleries in Duke Humfrey but no access to them from those in Arts End, the walls there being totally covered by bookcases. The staircases to the Arts End galleries shown in the engraving were removed towards the end of the 18th cent. and it is likely, therefore, that the apertures were made at that time to give access to those galleries by way of the staircases in the studies. This arrangement lasted until 1877 when the Duke Humfrey galleries and their staircases were removed for ever. From then until 1919, when the present replicas of the original staircases were installed, access to the Arts End galleries was, first, by ladders and then, from 1897, by unsightly spiral iron staircases. (BQR ii (1917–19), 172.)

41. MS Bodl. 907, fol. 7; Macray, p. 168. It is not clear exactly what was done under Aldrich's direction, but in a drawing by Robert Potter (Myres, fig. 3) are shown iron ties going through the walls to secure the wall-posts. They are attributed, in the drawing, to Wren but it seems more likely that they constitute Aldrich's work of 1693. The only ties proposed by Wren were the massive iron rods which were to brace opposite buttresses from side to side (but were not adopted) and the iron trusses to secure the standing bookcases to the walls, marked L in his plan (Ill. 24).

42. 5 March 1699/1700: MS Bodl. 907, fol. 4. Printed in J. Walker, *Oxoniana*, iii [1809], 16–18.

43. MS Bodl. 907, fol. 7. Reproduced in *Sir Christopher Wren: Bicentenary Memorial Volume* (1923), rear endpaper.

44. MS Bodl. 907, fol. 8. Reproduced in *Sir Christopher Wren*, inside rear cover. Printed in Walker, loc. cit. 18–20.

45. MS Bodl. 907, fol. 10. Printed in *Sir Christopher Wren*, but incorrectly, pp. 237–8.

46. MS Bodl. 907, fol. 11. Reproduced in *Sir Christopher Wren*, inside front cover. Printed in Walker, loc. cit. 20–4.

47. MS Bodl. 907, fols. 13, 14.

48. Robinson's drawing is not among the Wren papers in MS Bodl. 907. Upon the original folder (fol. 3) which housed them is a note in a contemporary hand referring to it: 'Perhaps never brought into the Library'.

49. MS Bodl. 907, fol. 15.

50. MS Bodl. 907, fol. 16.

51. MS Bodl. 907, fols. 17, 18.

52. MS Bodl. 907, fols, 21, 22. Printed in Walker, loc. cit. 25–7.

53. See G. M. Briggs, 'The general removal 1723', *BLR* iii (1950–2), 213–22.

54. Macray, p. 208.

55. See I. G. Philip, 'Reconstruction in the Bodleian Library and Convocation House in the eighteenth century', *BLR* vi (1957–61), 418–19.

56. Curators' Minutes, 7 June 1845 (Library Records d. 12, fol. 83^v).

57. Macray, pp. 310–11; Craster, p. 27.

58. *Pietas*, 10; Craster, p. 7.

59. Craster, p. 7.

60. *Pietas*, 10 n.

61. Galton's Report was published in the *Oxford University Gazette*, 20 Mar. 1877.

62. Craster, pp. 139–40.

63. Poole, i. 1.

64. Ibid. 2, 3.

65. For Taylor see ibid. i, pp. xxvii, xxviii; ii, pp. xiv, xv; iii, p. 349. From the east end, in a clockwise direction, the portraits represent John Balliol (no. 1); Dervorguilla Balliol (no. 3); Walter de Merton (no. 2); Walter de Stapledon (Exeter, no. 5); Edward II (Oriel, no. 6); Robert Eglesfield (Queen's, no. 7); William of Wykeham (New College, no. 10); Richard Fleming (Lincoln, no. 12); Henry Chichele (All Souls, no. 13); William Waynflete (Magdalen, no. 14); William Smith (Brasenose, no. 18); Richard Fox (Corpus Christi, no. 20); Henry VIII

(Christ Church, no. 31; given to the University by the college in 1769 in exchange for the portrait in the original series); Sir Thomas Pope (Trinity, no. 35; the portrait in the original series went to Trinity and this one was given to the University by the college in lieu); Sir Thomas White (St John's, no. 36); Elizabeth I (Jesus, no. 57); Dorothy Wadham (no. 78); Nicholas Wadham (no. 64); Thomas Tesdale (Pembroke, no. 65); Richard Wightwick (Pembroke, no. 87); Sir Thomas Cookes (Worcester, no. 181; by Michael Dahl, not part of the original series). The numbers refer to the descriptions in Poole, i.

66. *Annual Report, 1913.*

67. *Annual Report, 1920,* 21.

68. *Annual Report, 1957–8,* p. 4 and ill.

69. *Annual Report, 1921.*

70. *Annual Report, 1926; BQR* v (1926–8), 56–7.

71. *Annual Report, 1929.*

72. *BLR* i (1938–41), 210; *Annual Report, 1944–5,* 1.

73. *BLR* iv (1952), 289; *Annual Report, 1953–4,* 2.

74. *Annual Report, 1956–7,* 1.

75. Myres, *passim; BLR* vi (1957–61), 577–8, vii (1962–7), 1–2; W. F. Oakeshott (ed.), *Oxford Stone Restored* (1975), 21–9.

76. H. S. Scott (ed.), *The Journal of Sir Roger Wilbraham* (1902), 64. (Camden Soc., ser. 3, iv: Camden Miscellany, x).

INDEX